THE HOME TEAM:

My Bromance with Off-Brand Football

Published by Burnaby Books, an imprint of Burnaby, LLC

Burnaby titles may be purchased in bulk for educational, business, fund-raising or sales promotional use. For information please see www.burnabybooks.com.

Adamson, Scot (1960 -_
The Home Team: My Bromance with Off Brand Football/ by Scot Adamson
    1.   Sports, 2. Football Fans, 3. Southern Culture

Library of Congress Control Number: Pending
ISBN: 978-0-9796988-9-7

This book was printed in the United States of America.
1.0

The Home Team
My Bromance with Off-Brand Football

Scott Adamson

Burnaby Books

ACKNOWLEDGEMENTS

While I rely on my memory, old newspaper clippings (including some of my own), and vintage programs and media guides I've collected to recreate my experiences following Birmingham's professional football teams, I also owe a debt of gratitude to others who have kept defunct leagues alive through their own hard work.

Gene Crowley runs BirminghamProSports.com, which covers just about everything you'd want to know about professional sports history in the Magic City. Greg Allred is responsible for WFL1974.com, which pays tribute to the Americans and Vulcans. And wfl.charlottehornetswfl.com – a Richie Franklin production with Jim Cusano and Greg serving as consultants – is a gloriously detailed source of information for WFL geeks like me.

Knowing there are others who still carry the torch for teams and leagues that are gone but not forgotten (by us, anyway) makes me feel like I'm part of a unique community. Mostly I want to thank my wife, Mary, who convinced me to write this book, served as its main editor, and is the love of my life. This is for you.

TABLE OF CONTENTS

HOW IT ALL STARTED

On Sept. 22, 1968, Legion Field hosted its very first major professional football regular season game. "My" team was there, even though their home was roughly 1,000 miles away from my hometown of Birmingham, Alabama. My team, by the way, was (and still is) the New York Jets. They were in town serving as visitors against the "host" Boston Patriots in an American Football League Eastern Division clash; the Pats were having stadium issues (they shared Fenway Park with the Boston Red Sox), and decided to experiment with some home games played on the road. On this particular Sunday – the second week of the league's ninth season – Birmingham subbed for Beantown. Featuring former Alabama signal caller Joe Namath (my favorite quarterback), sure-handed wideout Don Maynard (my favorite wide receiver) and wearing green (my favorite color), the Jets had won my heart a year earlier when – for no reason I can adequately explain – I decided that tackle football was the greatest thing in the world.

More importantly, I decided the American Football League was the greatest version of the game I could hope for. While National Football League contests seemed more geared toward defense (at least to me), the AFL was wide-open from the opening whistle to the final gun.

Of course as a kid growing up in Birmingham, the University of Alabama and Auburn University were supposed to be your first football priorities. You had to pick a side, and Football Saturdays were deemed to be a lot more important than Football Sundays. Southern states such as Alabama, Tennessee, Mississippi, Arkansas, North Carolina and South Carolina had no NFL teams and placed all their football passion on the college game. That was true for most of my friends, but not for me. Yes, I followed the Crimson Tide and Tigers (cheering mostly for Paul "Bear" Bryant's Alabama team and, on occasion, jumping on Ralph "Shug" Jordan's Auburn bandwagon), but professional football seemed more exotic and compelling. Though the AFL was my play-for-pay circuit of choice, I also made room for the NFL, where I followed the Los Angeles Rams. I thought those horns on their helmets were fantastic and Roman Gabriel was second only to Namath in my personal QB rankings.

My dad was a Green Bay fan and had been since former Alabama wide receiver Don Hutson suited up for the club, and we had a friendly rivalry. We'd chart how the Packers and Rams were doing throughout the season and when it was over, one of us would claim bragging rights. When it came to the AFL, however, we were both "Team Jets."

Yet while Bama and Auburn were regular visitors to the stadium on Graymont Avenue, pro football would only parachute in on occasion for an exhibition. TV was as close as I could ever come to watching Broadway Joe connect with Sunshine on a long scoring play. Until this particular Sunday. Why I didn't beg Pop to take me to the game, I'll never know. If there was any way possible, I bet he would have. After five decades, it's really hard to remember details that might explain how he and I missed out on the chance to see our favorite AFL team in action. But I do remember reading about it – marveling that pro football had come to my hometown.

Looking at the black and white pictures on Monday I read about the contest told the story of a 47-31 Jets victory – one of 13 in a year that ended with a stunning Super Bowl III victory over the Baltimore Colts. The fact that the pro team I idolized had played a game in my backyard was thrilling – although as a 7 year-old kid I never dreamed Birmingham would have a pro team to call its own. And if you want to get technical, this was a real audition in terms of landing a major league pro team. Patriots owner Billy Sullivan had threatened to move his team if a suitable stadium wasn't built. In fact, as part of an impending merger with the NFL, which became official in 1970, each AFL team was required to have a venue that seated at least 50,000. That led AFL commissioner Milt Woodard to suggest the Patriots play a "test" game – which would be an actual regular season contest – somewhere else.

Legion Field was one of the top facilities in the United States. It was given the nickname "Football Capital of the South" when it was built in the late 1920s as a state-of-the-art stadium, and rapid expansion in the 1960s and marquee matchups helped it live up to the title. By 1965 it had undergone its second renovation, increasing capacity to 68,821 and further establishing its bona fides as one of the sport's most prestigious venues. Alabama had already claimed three national championships in the decade of the 1960s, and all of its key home games were played before sellout crowds at the municipal stadium. Knowing that, Sullivan decided to play a home game there against the Jets. If a big crowd showed up, it might be enough to convince him to take his team to the Deep South. "Frankly, we hope to get in the area of 50,000 customers," Patriots official Bob Hoobing told the Boston Globe in the lead up to the game. "We made the decision and announcement on the Birmingham game back in April. We couldn't guess whether or not Fenway Park would be tied up with a World Series and we couldn't wait until Oct. 13 for our first home game."

The pot was sweetened since Namath was quarterbacking the Jets. Surely that would entice mass numbers of Crimson Tide fans to pack the stadium. When he came to town back in 1966 for an exhibition game against the Houston Oilers, 57,305 fans showed up. At the time, that was the largest crowd to ever see an AFL preseason contest and just 4,000 below the all-time league record. Sadly – at least for those of us who longed

for an AFL or NFL team in the hub of the Cotton State
– Broadway Joe's appearance did not have the desired
effect on attendance this time. A day after 63,759 fans
watched Alabama beat Virginia Tech 14-7 at Legion
Field, only 29,192 made a return trip to the "Gray Lady"
to witness the Jets beat the Pats. "The Patriots suffered a
complete disappointment and Birmingham at least a
mild one," read an Associated Press account of the game
on Sept. 23, 1968. "Boston is having difficulty finding a
suitable playing site, and the game was billed as a test to
see how the AFL would draw in Birmingham. A crowd
of 29,129 turned out at Legion Field, which seats
70,000." Hugh Morrow III, who had spent several years
laying the groundwork for Birmingham pro football, had
hoped for – and expected – much better. "It points up
what we knew, that Birmingham is an Alabama
(football) town," Morrow told the Associated Press. "We
thought the Alabama game (played the night before at
Legion Field) would help us, with people staying over,
and in a way it has, but the economics of the thing enter
in. Many people apparently wouldn't buy tickets for
Saturday night and Sunday, too. They couldn't really
afford it."

If the Birmingham Patriots had been born of that
contest, you wouldn't be reading this book. But they
weren't, and you are. So, less than six years after New
York and Boston brought their insurgent league to
Legion Field, another upstart organization was in
business and Birmingham was a major part of it.
Although there were a few semi-pro leagues that came

before it, the World Football League of 1974 marked my city's first flirtation with what I consider "legitimate" professional football. And since that time, Birmingham has been a part of the United States Football League, World League of American Football, Canadian Football League, XFL, and the Alliance of American Football. That means I've had the chance to cheer for the Birmingham Americans and Vulcans (WFL), Fire (WLAF), Barracudas (CFL), Thunderbolts (XFL) and Iron (AAF). As a 30-year newspaper sports writing veteran, my job even overlapped with three of those leagues.

I'll also touch on the Alabama Vulcans (1979) and Alabama Magic (1982) of the minor league American Football Association. I don't have nearly as much to say about those two, but the AFA Vulcans and Magic both played a decent brand of football, far better than they're given credit for (and they deserve more credit than I gave them at the time). Plus, I won the "Name the Team" contest that resulted in the Magic – and received several fantastic prizes, including season tickets and a case of eggs. Spoiler alert: I got a lot more use out of the eggs.

I'm leaving out the Birmingham/Alabama Steeldogs (2000-07) of Arena Football League 2, though they were the longest-lasting pro football team in Birmingham history. No disrespect intended, it's just that indoor football is a whole 'nother animal and, frankly, I never followed the team. While I can reel off dates and scores of many Americans, Vulcans and Stallions games, I can tell you very little about the Steeldogs. About my only memory is covering their inaugural regular season game at the Birmingham-Jefferson Civic Center against the Tennessee Valley Vipers in 2000 (a 59-18 loss for the home team), which was highlighted by the late Mindy McCready singing the national anthem. That's about as deeply as I can dig into the Steeldogs, and for those who know me, that's surprising. I enjoy indoor soccer and indoor lacrosse, so one would think I'd have glommed onto indoor football. It just never happened.

My level of interest in the outdoor teams - and level of fandom - has varied over the years. The first team came along when I was 13 and the last debuted when I was 58. The Americans will always be my first love because, well, they were the first Birmingham team I had a chance to love - and they rewarded me with a championship. I can say without hesitation that my most cherished football memories revolve around the Ams, especially in the very early days of the franchise. The Vulcans were a repackaged version of the Americans, playing in a rebooted and reorganized WFL that didn't look nearly as promising as the league that debuted in 1974. But ... Pop bought $50 worth of stock in the team, so there was quite literally a sense of ownership there.

The Stallions, I think, were the most talented team this city has ever had; by their third and final year, they could've been competitive against many NFL clubs. I'm not saying they could've jumped to the established league and been a playoff contender, but they certainly wouldn't have been doormats. The USFL offered outstanding football, and Birmingham was one of its best teams in the end. We'll never know, of course, but I like to think if the USFL had stuck to a spring schedule it might still be around to today – and we'd be enjoying top shelf football year-round.

The Fire had the prestige and money of the NFL behind it, but as a developmental league, it didn't have the aspirations of the WFL and USFL. There is absolutely nothing wrong with minor league football – unless, of course, you aren't satisfied with anything short of a major league. In addition, they played 10-game regular seasons, which isn't nearly enough gridiron action for my tastes.

And the 'Cudas? Yeah, the American experiment ultimately failed, but I became a CFL fan 40 years ago and I was thrilled that my hometown was a part of it. By 1995 (the team's only year of existence) I thought I had shed all by naivety about pro sports, but since the CFL had been around for many years I assumed the Barracudas would last a while, too. While they didn't have the same "vibe" as the Americans, Vulcans and Stallions, they competed in a great league with exciting rule innovations, and didn't have to work to win my allegiance. I'll talk up the Canadian Football League all day long whether you want to hear about it or not.

As for the Bolts ... Vince McMahon's bluster made it hard for me to take the league seriously, especially since it tried to package football in the style of World Wrestling Entertainment. I followed it and tried to embrace it, but never could form the proper fan connection.

And the Iron, well, if you blinked you might've missed them. I wasn't crazy about the name, but I loved the logo, dug the silver and black colors, and vowed to follow them as a fan and as a "semi-pro" writer. Sadly, the Alliance of American Football folded eight weeks into its lone season. Like the WLAF and XFL, the AAF was designed as more of a second chance league than an NFL competitor and, in fact, hoped to become a developmental league for the kings of professional football. That hope died on April 2, 2019, when the league suspended operations and officially folded not long after.

The focus of this book isn't meant to be a dry, textbook-style chronicle of Birmingham's pro football history, full of stats and insider league minutiae. There's certainly plenty of that, and hopefully by the end of this book you'll be trivia-savvy when it comes to this town's pro football journey. But what I really want to share are my memories of what pro football in a non-NFL city means (and has meant) to me. I'm willing to bet there are at least a few of you out there who feel pretty strongly about the game and your town, too, and the idea is to jog some fond memories. Although I spent parts of four decades as a sports writer for newspapers in Alabama and South Carolina, I've spent most of my life as a sports fan. And through it all, no sport has impacted me more than football, and no football teams have fascinated me more than the ones that have called Birmingham home. This is primarily a love letter to them – and a bittersweet nostalgia trip that will accentuate the good times far more than the bad. I hope you'll tag along and enjoy taking this gridiron nostalgia trip with me.

THE WORLD FOOTBALL LEAGUE

The World Football League, formed on Oct. 3, 1973, lived fast, died young, and left a corpse drowning in red ink. If I wanted to, I could write volumes about one of the greatest financial disasters in American sports history. But I have no interest in treating it like a court case; I can't ignore it, but I don't have to make it the centerpiece of my memories. At the league's first news conference, WFL founder Gary Davidson announced that the six charter cities in his league would be Los Angeles/Anaheim, New York, Honolulu, Tampa and Tokyo, and six more would be added as investors came forward. Some of the other cities in the running included Chicago, Detroit, Mexico City, Boston, Milwaukee and Cleveland.

"The National Football League has been very successful," Davidson told United Press International. "They are established now. But we are going to try to loosen everybody up a little bit ... provide a bright new look to the sport. We are going to play with some different rules and open the game up." I read about the new league and was excited that there would be more football coming. However, it seemed like such a big, international venture that it never even occurred to me that Birmingham would or could be a part of it. But a couple of months later it was, and it would supposedly be part of a league willing to provide big paydays.

"We feel there are a number of people who would like to increase their income," Davidson said. "For some of the guys who feel like they're being paid less than they're worth, we'll try to balance out the inequities." When the WFL began play in July, 1974, I was 13 years old and my only concept of finance was how much money I could earn by cutting grass or doing odd jobs around the house. And I wasn't the least bit interested in how much franchises cost or what players made in this new league; I was just thrilled that Birmingham was in the professional football business. For the record, the inaugural WFL season started with 12 franchises: the Birmingham Americans, Chicago Fire, Detroit Wheels, Florida (Orlando) Blazers, (Honolulu) Hawaiians, Houston Texans, Jacksonville Sharks, Memphis Southmen, New York Stars, Philadelphia Bell, Portland Storm, and Southern California Sun.

"We know football is the biggest sports market in North America," WFL founder Gary Davidson told the National Post of Toronto in a November, 1973, interview. "You don't even need numbers to back that up. But it's virtually impossible to buy into the NFL, and the CFL doesn't want to expand. An NFL franchise now operating would cost about $20 million. We know there's room for another league, and we know it will go."

There were many false starts before that lineup was complete, which might've been a harbinger of the league's ultimate doom had anyone been paying closer attention. One of the founding franchises was supposed to be the Boston Bulls, but money woes prompted a merger with the New York club that would become the Stars. The Florida Blazers evolved from the Washington Ambassadors, which became the Washington-Baltimore Ambassadors and then the Virginia (Norfolk) Ambassadors before landing in Orlando and becoming the Orlando Suns, only to finally take the field as the Florida Blazers since Southern Cal was already nicknamed the Sun. The original Memphis franchise was moved to Houston, and the franchise that became the Memphis Southmen (the locals called them the "Grizzlies") started as the Toronto Northmen. However, the club received so much pressure from the Canadian government that Memphis owner John Bassett (who would later bring the World Hockey Association to Birmingham and become one of my favorite people in sports), opted to take the team south of the border and south of the Mason-Dixon line in May. Although the grand plan was to make the league global – eventually expanding to such exotic locales as Tokyo, London and Mexico City – at the outset it couldn't even figure out a way to expand its footprint to Canada.

So, the WFL was based entirely in the United States. Unlike the NFL, which had six exhibition games before embarking on a 14-game regular season, the WFL had no preseason contests outside of controlled scrimmages and played 20 regular season clashes from mid-July through November. Most games were slated for Wednesday nights, with a TV "Game of the Week" scheduled for each Thursday and syndicated throughout the nation on the TVS television network. Although the league started its season nearly two months before the NFL opened, playing on weeknights was a way to avoid competing with any other kind of football once season overlapped. In the earliest iteration of the WFL rulebook, it was stated that 2-point conversions were optional; only PATs were allowed in the NFL.

But then Davidson, also the league's original commissioner, and his rules committee decided that touchdowns themselves would be worth 7 points, with the idea that a TD ought to count more than a pair of field goals. And instead of an extra point teams would try an "action point" where they could score 1 point following a touchdown with a successful run or pass from the 2 and a half yard line. To this day, I still think those are two of the best rule innovations in all of football.

Other changes were:

- Kickoffs from the 30-yard line, a change designed to increase the likelihood of kick returns.
- Goal posts located at the back of the end zone.
- Missed field goals returned to the line of scrimmage except when attempted inside the 20-yard line.
- Only one foot in bounds required for a pass completion.

- In case of a tie at the end of regulation there would be a fifth quarter, divided into two 7 1/2 minute segments, to break ties.
- Fair catches would not be permitted on punts. Instead, the returner would receive a 5-yard cushion allowing him to field the kick.
- Offensive backs could go in motion toward the line of scrimmage before the ball is snapped.
- Hash marks were moved closer to the center of the field to give offenses more room to work.
- Any incomplete pass on fourth down would be returned to the line of scrimmage.
- Offensive holding would be a 10-yard penalty instead of 15.

Many of these rules are common practice today, but in 1974 they were revolutionary. The rules were designed to make the WFL an offensive-minded league, positioning itself as a more wide-open alternative to the NFL. It worked for the AFL, so why not the newbies? "We're competing with the NFL in playing quality," Davidson said during his interview with the National Post. "That means attracting high price talent, stars, big names."

BIRMINGHAM AMERICANS (1974)

When I learned Birmingham was going to be part of a new football league, it was lightly snowing. The date was December 20, 1973 – five days before Christmas and 11 days prior to my 13th birthday. I was monitoring the white stuff on one of the local television stations when it was reported that Davidson, who was co-founder of both the American Basketball Association and World Hockey Association, would make Birmingham one of the World Football League's charter franchises. I hadn't yet discovered ice hockey – a sport I'd become passionate about – but I loved the ABA and claimed the New York Nets as my favorite team, so Davidson certainly seemed like someone who knew how to get cool sports leagues up and running.

Birmingham had no nickname or no coach at the time, but it would have a team, and that team would begin play in the summer of 1974. I had seen Alabama and Auburn play at Legion Field and even watched a couple of high school games there, but never pro football. I was thrilled, and celebrated the glorious occasion by running out onto the snowy street – a football in hand – and playing toss with myself. The next morning I grabbed the Birmingham Post-Herald and read that the team would be owned by Atlanta businessman Bill Putnam.

"Birmingham has football interest, it has the stadium, and it's logical to me that pro football should be here," he said. In the coming days, weeks and months, I'm sure I irritated Pop to no end because all I could talk about or think about was Birmingham's team – one that would bring Tide and Tiger players together for the common good. What would be the team's nickname? (I was hoping for Birmingham Magicians because I lived in "The Magic City"). What would be our colors?

(Black, red and silver). Who would be the coach? (I wanted George Allen). How many Alabama and Auburn players will be on the roster? (Made no difference to me). When can we get tickets? (Pop promised to go to Legion Field and get tickets for the first home game as soon as they went on sale).

Every night I watched the 5 o'clock and 10 o'clock news in hopes of finding out new information about the new league, and each day I carefully dissected The Birmingham News and Birmingham Post-Herald for updates. Finally, as the winter morphed into the spring of 1974, everything was starting to come together. The team was nicknamed the "Americans" in late February, which I'm sure to those outside of Birmingham seemed to have nothing in particular to do with a town once known for its steel industry. Birmingham had been "The Magic City" for as long as I could remember, nicknamed that because of its impressive growth at the turn of the 20th century – growth that transformed it from a sleepy Southern town to a major industrial metropolis. It didn't take "All-America City" honors until the National Civic League bestowed the award in 1970 yet that was good enough, I suppose, to convince Putnam to give the club a star-spangled brand. It was less exciting for the WFL's Washington franchise. Word is its owners were hoping to call the team the Americans before playing musical cities and ultimately never playing a down anywhere near the District of Columbia.

As for the announcement of the Americans' first head coach, well, it took a while. Putnam's first choice was Vince Costello, who was an assistant coach with the Cincinnati Bengals but who wound up with the two-time defending Super Bowl champion Miami Dolphins as an assistant instead. "Let's put it this way," Costello told the Cincinnati Enquirer in April, 1974. "I was approached by the Birmingham people and I talked to them. It was before I took the job with Miami, or was even offered the job in Miami." I didn't think the Americans were going to lure Bryant or Jordan, of course, but maybe they could get an NFL head coach to jump ship. The reason I wanted George Allen is because he was my favorite NFL coach when he was with the Rams, and by 1974 he was in D.C. guiding the fortunes of Washington – a team I cared nothing about. With Costello out of the picture team officials looked north of the border to Canada, where they plucked Jack Gotta from the Ottawa Rough Riders of the Canadian Football League on February 5, 1974.

Gotta was at the height of his career when he decided to join the WFL. Only 43, the Michigan native was a rising star in the coaching ranks. After back-to-back losing seasons in his first two years in Ottawa (1970-71), Gotta guided the Riders to the playoffs in 1972 and won the Grey Cup – the CFL's version of the Super Bowl – in 1973. While I'd guess many fans in my hometown had no idea on earth who Gotta was, I did because I was already a fan of the CFL. When I mentioned that tackle football had become one of the most important things in my life back in 1967, the obsession extended beyond the United States. I spent as much time as I could reading everything there was to read about professional football, and the CFL had caught my fancy long before the WFL was a twinkle in Davidson's eye. There was even a period in the early 1970s when the local CBS affiliate showed truncated CFL games during Sunday nights in the summer. It was part of something called Tomorrow Syndication, Inc., and starting in 1972 the network struck a deal with 109 U.S. TV stations to shows 20 Wednesday night CFL games throughout the season.

While the games beamed to Birmingham were shown on a delayed basis, it was still football and I was all in. I rarely missed a game and was fascinated by the rules, which were quirky compared to what I was used to. I loved them, and still do. Three downs to make 10 yards, 12 players to a side, all backs other than the QB allowed in motion, wideouts racing toward the line of scrimmage before the snap, scoring a "rouge" – it's good stuff.

So although Gotta might not have been a big name in the U.S., he was already a big deal in Canada. He wasn't the "wow" hire I had originally hoped for, but he had championship credentials. I decided that just because he wasn't a household name in Birmingham didn't mean he couldn't become one, so his selection was just fine by me. (Shortly after he was hired, bumper stickers appeared around town that read, "Birmingham's Gotta Win." That was cute, but the coach's last name was pronounced "Goat-ah.")

As for the players, I thought the Americans did a nice job of mixing in NFL veterans with guys boasting local ties. Veteran quarterback George Mira would start ahead of strong-armed rookie backup QB Matthew Reed, and former NFL rushing stars Charley Harraway and Paul Robinson gave Birmingham some star power in the backfield. Mira never had a major impact in the NFL, playing for three different teams over seven seasons and managing just 19 touchdowns. During five seasons with the San Francisco 49ers he was the understudy to John Brodie, while in 1969 he split time with Norm Snead at Philadelphia and rode the bench with Miami in 1971 while Bob Griese ran the show. Before going to the WFL, he played two years with the Montreal Alouettes.

Reed had spent time in a pair of NFL camps, but both Buffalo and Denver wanted to convert him to tight end. Having starred at QB for Eddie Robinson at Grambling and earning both All-American and All-Southwestern Athletic Conference honors, Birmingham saw him as a versatile quarterback and someone who could challenge Mira for the starting job. In eight NFL seasons (three with the Cleveland Browns and five with the Washington Redskins), Harraway had amassed 3,019 yards and 20 touchdowns. Robinson made history in 1968 as the first player to gain more than a thousand rushing yards for a first-year expansion team when – as a rookie – he gathered up 1,023 for the Cincinnati Bengals. He finished his NFL run as a Houston Oiler in 1973.

The Ams also featured guard Buddy Brown, wide receiver Dennis Homan, defensive tackle Skip Kubelius, and defensive back Steve Williams from Alabama, while Auburn was repped by center Jay Casey and defensive back Larry Willingham. Homan and Willingham provided some homegrown star power: Homan was an All-American at Alabama and spent five seasons in the NFL, while Willingham was a two-time All-SEC selection out of Auburn and had a two-year stint with the St. Louis Cardinals. It was going to be an adjustment for fans who had spent their lives screaming either "Roll Tide!" or "War Eagle!" finding themselves on the same side. Really, though, the team could've been stockpiled with players from Timbuktu Tech and they would've had my complete and unconditional support.

It was my city. It was my team. And when it came to my "fandom," the Jets finally had some real competition.

PRESEASON

There were no exhibition games in the WFL, but there were controlled scrimmages. And the two the Americans played gave me every reason to be wildly optimistic about their chances in 1974. Their first came against the Jacksonville Sharks in Daytona Beach on July 29. Playing in front of 4,700 fans at Memorial Stadium, Birmingham was dominant in a 31-11 victory. Mira and third-string quarterback Denny Duron – a rookie out of Louisiana Tech who helped the Bulldogs win the 1973 NCAA Division II championship – each threw for touchdowns. Linebacker Ronald Foxx, an Alabama A&M product, had two interceptions in the contest and returned a blocked kick 63-yards for a score. The Americans led 23-0 at halftime and Jacksonville didn't score until the fourth quarter.

Just four days later Birmingham was on the field again, this time at its training camp at Marion Military Institute. With more than 4,000 fans looking on at David J. Robinson Memorial Stadium, Birmingham crushed the Houston Texans, 34-8. Mira and Reed split time behind center but Reed had the best day, throwing for two touchdown passes (one a 34-yarder). Robinson also scored a pair of rushing touchdowns and the Americans led 34-0 before Houston averted the shutout with a fourth quarter touchdown and action point. "Yes, I was somewhat surprised by the final score," Gotta told the Selma Times-Journal. "But I was well-pleased with the effort of our players, especially the defense."

OPENING NIGHT

By the time July 10, 1974, rolled around, I had already been to Legion Field many, many times in my life. My first trip to what I considered football's grand cathedral was on Sept, 19, 1970, when Pop took me to see the Virginia Tech Hokies (then better known as the VPI Gobblers) take on Alabama. The Tide won, 51-18. Two years later on September 23, 1972, Pop, my mom and I went to the Alabama-Kentucky game at Legion Field, which ended in a 35-0 victory for Bama. The headline there was the fact that my mother tagged along. That seemed out of character for someone who had zero interest in sports, and to the best of my knowledge it was a one-and-done experience for her.

During the 1973 season, I was on hand to watch Auburn edge Oregon State, 18-9. The date was September 15 and the game was part of a rare stadium doubleheader that would see Alabama host California later that night. That was the game I really wanted to see but it was already a hard sellout (the Tide rewarded the capacity crowd with a 66-0 destruction of the Golden Bears). Being herded into college games at Legion Field meant you were awash in a sea of crimson and white or blue and orange. But 10 months later, a whole new world of football wonder – colored red, white and blue – was about to open.

This was the first time I'd been to the stadium to watch a professional football game, and to this day that date and everything that about the experience remains remarkably vivid.

My posse included Pop, my brother, Don, and his brother-in-law, Dave. We arrived at Legion Field right around 6 p.m. – approximately two hours before kickoff of the Southern California Sun vs. Birmingham Americans. My first order of business when we walked into the stadium was to buy a program. I had already become something of a program hoarder, and this one would become one of my most prized possessions. Looking at it now, I see a photo of Davidson, apparently in his commissioner's office, holding a mustard yellow football with powder blue stripes, while posters of all 12 of the teams' uniforms hung on a wall behind him. Being the goob that I am, I was most impressed by the football itself; I had never seen anything quite like it. Except for those orange-ish Hutch footballs we'd sometimes get as a kid, a pigskin was supposed to be brown. Next stop was the souvenir stand, where I promptly bought a Birmingham Americans pennant. Just like the program, I still have it today – and I'm quite impressed with myself that I've managed to keep it so nice and clean after more than 40 years. The most memorable pregame moment came not in what I bought, though, but where we sat.

We were between the 40 and 50-yard lines – upper deck side – sitting about 15 rows up. I had never come close to seats that good. I think the best I had ever scored was somewhere near the 20 – usually I was in the end zone. Even though the high roller seats made me feel like royalty, I'd have been content had I been stuck on top of the scoreboard. I was at a big-time football game with a big-time atmosphere, so just being there was enough.

The smells of fresh popcorn and hot dogs were unmistakable and unforgettable, and nothing tasted better than watered down Coca-Colas served from sweating, red and white cups. This was shaping up to be one of the most exciting days of my life, made even more exciting when I saw Southern Cal trot onto the field for warm-ups. Oh, don't get me wrong – I was firmly in the Americans' corner and they would get my full-throated support once the contest began – but man, the Sun was stylish. Wearing magenta jerseys, orange pants and white helmets with a hip sun-shaped logo, their look was one of the most 1970s things ever. The only thing missing from their sartorial splendor were bell bottom pants.

When Birmingham players burst onto the artificial turf, they looked regal in their home whites – blue numbers with red trim and stripes appointed similarly. And their logo, to me, remains timeless; an "A" designed to look like the American flag. But just as I grew comfortable with the colorful threads of the competing teams, I noticed something weird; the football they were playing with was not the football on the cover of my program. It was mustard yellow (I think officially it the color is called Palomino yellow), but instead of bluish stripes they were bright orange. By comparison this football looked better, but I didn't understand why it was not the same ball the commish was holding. Worrying about such a minor detail is ridiculous, of course, and I had to let it go at some point. That point came at 8 p.m., when the World Football League kicked off in front of more than 40,000 paying customers at the 68,821-seat venue. The moment toe met leather, the WFL became my favorite football league on the planet.

BIRMINGHAM HAS A WINNER

I had complete confidence that Birmingham would not only prevail in their WFL opener, but dominate. Truth be told, though, the opening game was hardly the most exciting gridiron battle ever waged, especially for a league that billed itself as one sure to keep the scoreboard technicians busy. Birmingham's attack spat and sputtered, managing just 241 yards on the night while being victimized by four interceptions. In fact, the Americans never even mustered an offensive touchdown; their only paydirt strike came when Williams intercepted a Tony Adams pass and returned it 50 yards for a touchdown to tie the game at 7-all early in the fourth quarter.

A successful action point made it an 8-7 game (Mira passed to Robinson for the score), and a 26-yard field goal by Earl Sark with under two minutes remaining put the tally at 11-7. Not a rollicking offensive showcase by any stretch of the imagination but the Ams still won, 11-7.

In retrospect, that pick six by Williams still ranks as one of my all-time favorite plays as a fan.

"The crowd – well, let's just say I was pleasantly surprised," Gotta told the Gadsden Times after the game. "You know, I kinda felt like we were like a little kid in an incubator before tonight and the people and the press gave us a chance to get out. Now I feel like we've got our legs under us and maybe we can really give the folks something to be proud of." Williams – the game's hero – agreed. "The crowd was really behind us, and that helped." he said. "This is going to be a good team ... a good town. They're good football fans." I suppose if I had been a more critical fan I would've picked quite a few nits with the Americans' debut, but I wasn't. And I didn't. A rough-around-the-edges beginning could be forgiven. Bottom line is that for the first time in my life, my city had a professional football team. To me, that was all that really mattered.

ROAD MIRACLE

Week two of the Ams' schedule took them to New York, where they faced the Stars at dimly-lit Downing Stadium. As a Jets fan, I kinda/sorta adopted the Stars as my "alternate" team, mainly because they had a few former Fly Boys on their roster, including three who played in Super Bowl III. The most famous was George Sauer, who was my second favorite receiver behind Maynard and was actually the AFL's leading pass catcher in 1967 – the year I became a fan of the sport, league and team.

The defense was led by Gerry Philbin and John Elliott, men who had a hand in the Jets' 16-7 world title win over Baltimore. On a Wednesday night in Randall's Island, however, I wished George, Gerry, John and their teammates nothing but the worst as Birmingham tried to go 2-for-2 in its pro football history. Things did not start off well for the visitors.

New York, which lost to Jacksonville, 14-7, in the league's first TV Game of the Week, jumped all over Birmingham and threatened to run Gotta's team out of the stadium. At halftime, the Stars' lead was 29-3, and I had completely given up. I started listening to the game on my transistor radio while playing with friends in the front yard, but this revolting turn of events caused me to retreat into the house. Once inside I spied Pop – armed with his ever-present cup of coffee and Lucky Strikes – soaking in the carnage on a clock radio situated on top of the television. I think I retreated to my room for a bit and listened to music (at the time I had Grand Funk's "The Loco-Motion" on a 45 and had almost worn it out by summer), not wanting to hear any more about the beat down. Then came a knock on my door.

"Bud, are you listening to the game?" Pop asked.

"No, sir," I said. "They're gettin' killed so I gave up."

"You might want to come in here and listen to it with me," Pop said with a smile. "I think you gave up too soon." Man, did I ever.

The Americans cut the lead to 29-15 after three quarters, giving me reason for hope. By the time the final horn sounded, Birmingham had finished the game on a 29-0 run, capped off by a 63-yard Mira-to-Homan TD connection late in the game to put the tally at 32-29 in favor of the Red, White and Blue. Mira told United Press International after the game there was really nothing miraculous about the comeback. "It was really a matter of my receivers getting used to the poor lighting," Mira said.

New York actually had a chance to tie the game with a field goal in the waning seconds and force overtime. However, the kick was off the mark and when Birmingham radio play-by-play man Larry Matson made the call, I unleashed a ridiculously loud yell and leapt straight into the air. It was probably the first time in my life Yogi Berra's old saying, "It ain't over 'til it's over" had any tangible meaning in my life, but it taught me that when it came to the Birmingham Americans football was, indeed, a 60-minute game.

When I woke up the next morning and read the accounts of the thriller, I was firmly convinced that Birmingham was the best team in the WFL and couldn't wait to see them again. Fortunately, I didn't have to wait long; my brother bought tickets to the rivalry showdown with the Memphis Southmen for July 24, and I was headed back to Legion Field for the second time in two weeks. I had no way of knowing it, of course, but not only would that game be one of the most exciting I've

ever witnessed, I also learned that football had the power
to bring people together.

RIVALRY NIGHT

The states of Alabama and Tennessee have been
football rivals for about as long as the sport existed. Back
in the days before conference expansion in college
football, Alabama and Auburn each played Tennessee
annually, with the Crimson Tide and Volunteers
meeting each season on the third Saturday in October in
a clash that was not only a storied one in the
Southeastern Conference, but one of the great rivalries
in football. Considering the WFL had only been playing
for three weeks, you couldn't quite classify the game
between the Americans and Southmen as a traditional
rivalry. But with nearly 60,000 fans jamming into
Legion Field to watch a battle of unbeaten teams, it
certainly had the feel of a really big deal.

Memphis was led by quarterback John Huarte, a
1964 Heisman Trophy winning quarterback out of
Notre Dame. He had spent time as a backup for
Namath with the Jets before playing a couple of seasons
with the Patriots and then knocking around the NFL
with three different teams. The Southmen also had a
great running back in J.J. Jennings, a rookie from
Rutgers who led the NCAA in scoring during his senior
season with the Knights. I was nervous before the game,
especially considering that Birmingham had to pull a
rabbit out of its helmet to beat New York a week earlier.

Those nerves morphed into energy after I entered the stadium.

Having been to several college games I was used to "electric" atmospheres, but this was unlike anything I had ever experienced. Long before kickoff the crowd was loud and proud, and by the time Don, Dave and myself squeezed into our seats under the upper deck (near the 20-yard line, roughly 60 rows up), fans were already well-lubricated. Sitting directly in front of us were two African-American men – Jimmy and Max – who quickly struck up a conversation with Don and Dave.

I was fortunate in that I grew up in a household that stressed treating everyone with respect, so whatever belief system I had developed at age thirteen and a half didn't include racism. That being said, I lived in an all-white neighborhood, went to an all-white grammar school and except for a handful of teachers, had never really been around black people in social situations. What I realized fairly quickly on this night, though, was that Jimmy and Max were a couple of really nice guys who – like me – had already fallen helplessly and hopelessly in love with the Americans. Max had been a fan of the NFL Atlanta Falcons since that city got an expansion team in 1966, but had switched loyalties once the Magic City had its own pro football team. Jimmy said he was a big college football fan and didn't really watch the pros much, but went to the WFL opener against Southern California, and became hooked. Anyone who watches sports knows it's a lot more fun when the people around you are having a good time, and this was already a party before the game ever kicked off. When it finally did, the party became a celebration.

I've seen a lot of football games in my life – many as a fan and even more while working at newspapers. And I've lost count of how many I've watched at Legion Field. I was in the stadium when Van Tiffin made "The Kick" to lead Alabama to a 25-23 victory over Auburn in the 1985 rivalry game in Birmingham, and I was in the press box when the Crimson Tide defeated the Tigers 31-17 at the last Iron Bowl ever played on Graymont Avenue in 1998. I've been fortunate to see a lot of great games there in my time. And from the standpoint of spell-binding drama and skill, I'm sure there were many that were technically "better" than this fracas between Birmingham and Memphis. But if I have to pick my favorite game of all time – college or pro and regardless of venue – it would be Birmingham 58, Memphis 33. The contest featured 957 yards of total offense, nine turnovers, and 242 penalty yards, but oh, my goodness what a fun night that was.

Birmingham built a 28-11 halftime lead and looked to have the game well in hand, only to see Memphis close the gap to 36-26 with a quarter left to play. But the Americans won the final 15 minutes, 22-7, and made the final score look like the game was a blowout. "I thought we had a good night offensively but there were far too many penalties," Gotta told UPI. "We've got to correct that because we can't keep winning making so many mistakes. We felt after watching the films that we could throw on Memphis. Their defensive backs came up and challenged the run, and so we sent Homan and Jenkins into the seams and were pretty lucky to get them open." Reed's first play of the night – in relief of Mira in the third quarter – was a 52-yard touchdown pass to Jenkins. "Coach Gotta called the play when he sent me in," Reed, who engineered three second half touchdowns, told the Anniston Star. "No, I wasn't surprised he told me to throw. I really didn't see the catch ... I got busted pretty good when I turned it loose." Reed had 200 yards in catches and three scores.

"With George out I though the fellows might lack a little confidence in Reed, but it sure didn't show," Jenkins said. "That man ... he doesn't need the confidence. He has his own." The win left Birmingham, Chicago and Florida as the only teams remaining in the league with perfect records. (As a side note I also got to see Danny White spell Huarte for a few plays. White, of course, was Roger Staubach's successor with the Dallas Cowboys and went on to have a solid NFL career). It was fast, it was furious, and one play in particular will always stand out for me. Reed's first TD pass to Jenkins in the third quarter prompted Max to turn around, pick me up, and toss me in the air. Fortunately, he caught me on the way down, and I remember our entire section of Legion Field suddenly looked like an impromptu street party. That was memorable enough, but the score also had a more profound effect; it allowed Jenkins to supplant Maynard as my favorite pass receiver. "I just played like I always play and like I always practice," Reed told The Anniston Star. "The first time I touched the ball I knew it was going to be my night." I would later choose Jenkins' number – 80 – as my own when L.M. Smith School began its YMCA football season in September.

It's funny how things that to some might seem like little more than a blink in time are so important. July 24, 1974, is seared into my memory. I'll always remember that game for being so exciting, but I'll always remember the experience more because that's the night I realized good people come in all shapes, sizes and colors. It was an object lesson in brotherhood, and one that I haven't forgotten.

PERFECT 10

I would've loved to have gone to every Americans home game, but the path to wealth did not run through the grass cutting business. And since school was about to start and my source of income was about to be reduced, I had to pick and choose. A week after the big win over Memphis, Birmingham traveled to Detroit to take on the Wheels. The WFL's Motor City-based club was already 0-3 and I figured the Ams would cruise. They didn't. Mira was out with an ankle injury and was sidelined by Reed, who had to use his legs to score a late go-ahead touchdown, allowing Birmingham to escape with a 21-18 victory.

"I approached this game, and our team did, with that worried feeling that if we didn't take it to them early they'd be tough to handle," Gotta told the Associated

Press. "I was right there. We were flat early and I think it was rather obvious Matthew Reed was a little tight when he started. He had some problems early, but he stuck in there like they all did." Due to a scheduling quirk, the Wheels were scheduled to come to Birmingham the very next week. Instead of saving ticket money for the clash with the Hawaiians on Aug. 14, I decided to go ahead and check out the rematch, hoping the Americans could prove that the close call was a fluke. Turns out, it wasn't a fluke at all. In fact, the game in Birmingham – played in front of more than 40,000 fans – was eerily similar to the battle waged seven days earlier.

Detroit led 22-20 with the clock winding down, and the Ams found themselves in desperate situation with only one drive left. But the Reed and Jenkins combo proved to be the difference, with the pair connecting on a 17-yard touchdown play with just 26 seconds remaining. It was another thrilling moment in a young season that had already provided quite a few, and it was money well spent.

Sure, it meant I'd have to miss the game against Hawaii, marking the first time Birmingham had been at Legion Field and I had not been there to watch, but I'd get over the disappointment. After all, this team was here to stay, right? I'd have the rest of my life to get up close and personal with my team. The only negative was a story that appeared in papers across the country that day. Although Davidson had told team officials to keep a lid on it, it turns out a lot of teams were "papering the house." I knew Birmingham was drawing big crowds to

Legion Field, and fans were showing up in large numbers at other league stadiums as well. But many were getting in at the low, low cost of absolutely nothing. The Philadelphia Bell were the primary offenders, with Bell executive vice president Barry Lieb admitting that of the 120,253 fans who attended their first two home games, more than 100,000 didn't pay a dime. "We just had to do it or we would've been a joke," Lieb told the Associated Press. "I admit we lied to everyone. What can I say – I never thought those figures would come out. It was what we had in mind the whole time. The first game, of course, was by design. I mean, to have people in the house. Then the second game was on TV, and how would it have looked if no one was there."

It was publicity the WFL didn't want or need and a more discerning person might've seen it as cause for alarm. But I was still on a Birmingham high, and quickly turned my attention to the Hawaiians. That game was a 39-0 blowout and a trip to Jacksonville on Aug. 21 ended in a 15-14 Birmingham victory. WFL games were syndicated by the TVS Network, and Birmingham finally got its chance to shine in the national spotlight on Thursday, Aug. 29, when it traveled to Soldier Field to meet the Chicago Fire. I had watched all of the televised WFL games religiously, but it was especially cool to finally see the Americans – who wore white uniforms at home – donning blue shirts against their Central Division rivals. By now Birmingham was the league's only unbeaten team, and that didn't change as Gotta's men left the Windy City with a 22-8 win. Birmingham

followed with two consecutive home games, and I had a
financial decision to make. Do I watch them play the
Florida Blazers on Sept. 2 – a Monday night (as well as a
"school night") – or save up for the Sept. 7 rematch
against Chicago, which would mark the first Saturday
game in Birmingham pro football history? I picked
Saturday, which turned out to be a good move.

The Monday game was probably the least exciting
the Ams had played to date, although the Legion Field
tenants escaped with an 8-7 victory after going scoreless
for three quarters. Reed, though still technically a
backup to Mira, had become the fan favorite behind
center, and ultimately led the way to win number nine. In
fact, Mira was being booed before finally being replaced
by the "understudy." "The crowd didn't bother me," Mira
told The Lakeland Ledger. "I'm out there to play football
... I can't pay any attention to the crowd." Reed tallied
Birmingham's lone touchdown on a short run, and
hooked up with tight end Jim Bishop on the action point
to provide the margin of victory. Yet while that game
was lacking in wire-to-wire thrills, the second encounter
with the Fire was incredible. The game was played in a
driving rainstorm due to remnants of Hurricane
Carmen, so I guess I should've been miserable from a
comfort standpoint.

My inclement weather attire of choice was a cheap,
bright orange poncho but honestly, I don't think it did a
bit of good. Instead of deflecting the rain it seemed to
absorb and then redistribute it. Not only that, but as a
kid who wore glasses, keeping my lenses dry long

enough to see what was happening on the field was a
challenge in itself. I don't remember how I kept them dry
but I obviously did because without them, I can't see
three feet in front of me. Lastly, I was nursing some
aches and pains by the time I got to the stadium. I had
played my first 8th grade football game of the 1974 season
that day, and got knocked around pretty good, including
a helmet to the kneecap on an end around play. But, I
had scored a 2-point conversion in L.M. Smith's
"thrilling" 20-14 victory over Huffman Elementary, so I
was in good spirits.

I was in an even better mood because Pop decided
he would join Don, Dave and I at the game, marking the
first time he'd been back to Legion Field since the season
opener. A small, thin man, I still chuckle when I think
about him rocking an oversized, old school yellow
raincoat and hood. He looked like Junior from the old
Foghorn Leghorn cartoon.   Funny thing is, I don't
remember any of us complaining about the torrential
downpour. And really, it was the sidebar to the main
story, which was that of one wild and thoroughly
enjoyable football game. From a statistical standpoint
Chicago's Virgil Carter was clearly the star of the game,
throwing five touchdown passes and amassing 309 yards
through the skies.   His favorite target was James Scott,
who reeled in three of his TD tosses and finished with
162 yards on 11 receptions. But as they had done nine
times before, Birmingham found a way to win – this time
to the tune of 41-40. After grabbing a nice early lead and
giving it away, Birmingham found itself trailing 40-38

with 52 seconds remaining. But despite the dicey wind and driving rain, Earl Sark drilled a 34-yard field goal to give the Ams the lead and, ultimately, the victory.

"This was the worst one of them all, from the point of thinking you had it won and almost losing it," Gotta told the Selma-Times Journal. "Virgil Carter picked us apart there for a while when we gave him time to throw. I was really pleased there early with the way we were moving the ball and the way things were happening and then wham – the bottom seemed to fall out on us. They really fought back." It was yet another joyous night in the confines of the "Gray Lady," despite getting so wet that I ruined a perfectly good pair of Converse sneakers and spent the next month sneezing. Yet I was joined by more than 50,000 people who chose football over health – at least for a night. "The fans were simply fantastic," Gotta said. "Where else would you see 54,000 people sit in a rainstorm and watch a football game?" Oh, and it should be noted that the song "The Night Chicago Died" by Paper Lace was played over the loudspeaker throughout the game. At the time, I pretended to enjoy it. I can tell you now I hate that freakin' song and ask that we never speak of it again.

REALITY CHECK

I'm not saying Birmingham's beatdown at the hands of Memphis in Week 11 was what caused me to remove my mustard yellow-colored glasses when it came to the WFL, but it came at a time when there seemed to be a lot of negative news surrounding the upstart league. As I said at the outset, when the WFL was formed I didn't think of it as a business, I thought of it as a new opportunity for football players to play football for my amusement. But I was already a voracious reader, and reading everything I could about Davidson's organization meant finding out things I didn't particularly want to know. More news broke about free ticket distribution – even in Birmingham. There was also deep financial trouble in New York, Jacksonville, Orlando, Houston and Detroit, with rumors that those franchises could move or fold. The biggest red flag seemed to be in Detroit, where players weren't being paid. A report in the Houston Post on September 10 said the Wheels franchise was set to move to Shreveport, where it would make a splash by signing Pittsburgh Steelers legend Terry Bradshaw and hiring South Carolina's Paul Dietzel as head coach. Turns out red flags were flying everywhere, and many players were working without compensation. It was years later before I could appreciate it, of course, but when you do a job – even a cool job like playing professional football – getting paid is an integral part of it. But I couldn't concern myself with that too much on Sept. 11, 1974; the Americans were about to mix it up with the Southmen in the Liberty Bowl, and Pop and I gathered in the living room to listen to it on what we called the "big radio." It was not a fun night.

While Birmingham had pulled rabbits out of hats time and time again through its first 10 games, the Ams were simply road kill on this night. Gotta's charges never led, trailed 22-7 at halftime, and entered the final 15 minutes on the sad end of a 30-7 score. By the time the Southmen added 16 unanswered points in the fourth quarter to complete a 46-7 demolition, I had already sulked off to my room and gone to bed. Receiver Ed Marshall was a one-man wrecking crew for the winners, reeling in TD passes covering 48, 12 and six yards. He also downplayed his team's earlier setback to the Ams at Legion Field. "I thought we were better than Birmingham the first time we played them," Marshall told the Associated Press. "We just weren't together then."

The perfect season was over, and the Americans had proven to be mortal. "I can't explain the one-sided loss to Memphis," Gotta told the Selma Times-Journal six days after the thrashing. "I just hope it was one of those bad games everyone will have, and that we got it out of our system." Birmingham rebounded with a 42-14 thrashing of Houston, but then suffered back-to-back losses to Portland (26-21) and the Hawaiians (14-8). The Ams avenged the loss to the Storm with a 30-8 victory before losing to Southern Cal, 29-25, in Anaheim on Oct. 16. On October 23 Birmingham's game at Shreveport was being televised, and Pop asked if I was going to watch it with him. I declined, opting instead to go up the street to a friend's house and shoot baskets with the radio broadcast serving as background music. Birmingham lost, 31-0. The sad part is, it didn't really even bother me. The Americans did close out the regular season on a roll, beating Florida (26-18), Philadelphia (26-23) and Shreveport (40-7), but the entire league was in shambles.

The New York Stars, in a prized media market and a team that arguably had more marquee value than any of the other 12 franchises, relocated to Charlotte after 13 games. Before morphing into the Hornets, they were known as the Charlotte Stars – slapping a "C" over the star logo in one of the greatest instances of slapdash rebranding in sports history. The "C," by the way, was the same style as the one used on Chicago Bears helmets. Houston, meanwhile, wasn't drawing well at all. So the Texans moved east and became the Shreveport Steamer.

Detroit and Jacksonville folded outright on October 10. The Wheels had declared bankruptcy three weeks earlier and were $2 million in debt, while Sharks players had been paid only once in the seven weeks leading up to the team disbanded.

There were also questions about whether or not the Fire and Blazers had enough income to make it to the end of the season. After such a promising start, there were now legitimate questions surrounding the league. Namely, would it even make it to the finish line? I'd love to tell you I was able to shrug off all the negativity and continue to be a true (red, white and) blue fan the rest of the way. I'd be lying. It wasn't just the league that was flailing ... so was my interest. I never went to Legion Field to see the Americans the rest of the season, and listening to games on the radio was done more out of a sense of obligation rather than true enthusiasm. It was like a switch had suddenly been flipped, and all the joy and excitement I had for "my" team had been unceremoniously drained.

WORLD BOWL ONE (AND ONLY)

By the time the WFL playoffs began, football had become a mixed bag for me. My 8th grade team had just wrapped up a 3-5-1 campaign, where in my role as starting wide receiver, kicker and backup quarterback, I had done a fine job contributing to our losing record. The Jets were putting together a bit of a winning streak, but it didn't really matter since they started the season 1-7. On the plus side Alabama and Auburn were both doing well; the Crimson Tide finished the regular season unbeaten and both schools were ranked in the Top 10. As for the Americans, well, I wasn't sure from day to day if they were even going to be around once I realized the WFL was on shaky ground. The wide-eyed enthusiasm I had as a kid who was thirteen and a half had faded now that I was a grizzled (almost) 14-year old, and I didn't want to waste my emotions. To show how weird things had gotten as the season stumbled to the end, the Hornets declined to even compete in the playoffs, and over the course of a few days the number of teams involved in the postseason went from six teams to four teams and then back to six teams. Oh, and Davidson resigned – under pressure – as commissioner on Oct. 29. When the inventor has to abandon his invention, it's never a positive development. Finally, though, a playoff system was agreed upon. Memphis (17-3) and Birmingham (15-5) received first round byes, while Florida (14-6) and Philadelphia (8-11) met in one quarterfinal and Southern Cal (13-7) and the Hawaiians (9-11) in the other. The Blazers edged the Bell to earn the right to play Memphis, while the Hawaiians surprised the Sun to get a shot at Birmingham.

The way the Southmen had finished the season they were fully expected to make quick work of their playoff foes. Once they defeated Florida at the Liberty Bowl, they'd host the Birmingham-Hawaii winner and walk away with the spoils.

However, things didn't turn out that way. The Blazers pulled off a stunner, upsetting Memphis, 18-15, at the Liberty Bowl.

The Americans, meanwhile, hung on to top the Hawaiians, 22-19, in front of just over 15,000 fans at Legion Field. That gave Birmingham the host spot for the title bout. Still, there was some question about whether or not the WFL championship game would even be played. By the time Birmingham and Florida were the last teams standing in the WFL, the Americans had gone eight weeks without getting paid and the poor Blazers had not received money in 14 weeks. On the Monday of World Bowl week (December 2) Birmingham players refused to practice and the threat that the game would be canceled was very real. On Tuesday, however, the Ams were back on the practice field. "We're not playing for back pay – we're playing for the championship," Harraway told the Associated Press.

"And, we're playing for the citizens of Birmingham and our pride." None of this seemed fitting for a major professional league. It didn't seem fit for any kind of league, period. Not only was the WFL bleeding money, it was becoming something of a laughingstock. Whatever the case – and despite the dark clouds hanging over the league – Birmingham would play for a championship, and they'd get to do it at home on Dec. 5.

This, I didn't expect. I mean, I wasn't surprised the Ams had bested the Hawaiians, but I surely thought they'd be playing the Southmen for the crown and the game would take place in Memphis. So the Football Capital of the South was going to be the Football Capital of the World (Football League) for one night and one night only, and I would be there to see it. Except I wouldn't be. While I had rolled the dice with my grass-cutting money in an effort to see the "best" Americans games during the first half of the season, I had squandered my earnings on albums the rest of the summer (the debut LPs by Rush and Kiss and Steely Dan's "Pretzel Logic" were worth it). And my funds were limited during the winter, so I had to be both stingy and highly selective with my entertainment cash. Long story slightly shorter, in November – when it appeared the WFL was in a death spiral – I never even thought about saving up to see another Birmingham game. Instead, I had the opportunity to buy a ticket to the 1974 Iron Bowl, featuring No. 2 and undefeated Alabama and No. 7 and once-beaten Auburn.

I had never been to a Tide-Tigers clash in person. And if you're a football fan in the Cotton State and you have the opportunity to attend this rivalry, you should probably do that. So I did that. Securing the ducat pretty much wiped me out, but that was fine because I'd finally get to witness – up close and personal – what many consider to be the fiercest rivalry in college football (in this renewal of the series Alabama won, 17-13). If memory serves, I had ticket in hand on Wednesday, November 20. A week later, Birmingham won its semifinal game and earned the right to host the World Bowl. Missing out on what still ranks (to me, anyway) as the biggest game in Birmingham pro football history haunts me to this day. And I really wonder what decision I would've made had I known the Americans were going to play for a league championship at home. Would I have still opted for the Iron Bowl, which was a huge deal but one that repeated itself annually, or would I have put my money down on a historic first?   Unless Doc Brown loans me his DeLorean and enough plutonium to generate the 1.21 gigawatts needed to travel back to 1974, we'll never know. However, I still got to see Birmingham win the title, although it was in front of a television set. The game was blacked out in Birmingham, but my brother lived in Center Point, a suburb that – for reasons I do not know – "got cable" before the Magic City had access to the television innovation. That meant getting programming from such exotic channels as WOR in New York - and it also meant picking up a TVS telecast of the World Bowl from an Atlanta station. So while I was still kicking myself for not jumping back on the Birmingham bandwagon one more time at Legion Field, at least Pop, Don and I could cheer from a living room in the 'burbs. It was a fun night.

The Americans jumped out to a 22-0 lead, using a punishing ground game with touchdown runs by Joe Profit and Art Cantrelle (and an action point jaunt by Reed) to grab a 15-0 advantage at the half. "Our guys were so cranked up and ready to play," Gotta told The Anniston Star. "But I knew those 15 points wouldn't stand up." Their final score came when Mira connected with Bob Brown on a 26-yard TD connection in the third quarter. At that point I was ready to celebrate, but the hosts had to hold off a furious Florida rally. The Blazers scored 21 unanswered points and appeared to have tied the game when Tommy Reamon went over the top for an action point following a 76-yard punt return courtesy of Rod Foster. Fortunately for the home fans, officials ruled Reamon had been stopped short of the goal line, and I wasn't about to argue with them. When the scoreboard finally hit double zeroes, it was the Americans hoisting the World Bowl Trophy with a 17-5 record.

I'm not sure how prevalent fist pumps were back in 1974, but I at least did my part to make them a thing as the final seconds ticked away. For the first time since that wet and wonderful game against Chicago, I felt excitement and joy when I realized what my team had accomplished. For one night, I wasn't worried about red ink or folded franchises or whether the WFL would even exist in the morning. The Birmingham Americans brought professional football to Birmingham, and they brought Birmingham a championship, too. You couldn't ask for much more than that.

"I don't know what happens tomorrow," Gotta said. "All I know is that tonight is the greatest thrill of my life." Thinking back on it decades later, it's even more special. These guys who represented both Birmingham and Florida hadn't been paid in weeks and had every reason to walk away and let their lawyers sort out the details. Instead, they played because they loved the game. They played for pride. And I still like to think that even though I didn't hold up my end of the bargain as a true fan, they played for me. I'll always love them for that. "A lot of real excellent players dedicated themselves, paying a high price on all those hot days," Gotta told The Anniston Star. "And our defense did an excellent job – we were playing a real good football team. This night will live long in their memories. In mine, too."

RED, WHITE AND BLUES

Even as the Americans celebrated the ascension to the top of the World Football League, Jefferson County sheriff's deputies were already confiscating helmets, jerseys and other equipment in the locker room. While the team was a success on the field and at the box office (in fairness attendance began to drop dramatically when the WFL started taking on water) it – like many other franchises in the league – had trouble paying its bills. The day after the World Bowl, the New York Times reported the WFL was already planning to reorganize, hoping to find at least six new club owners willing to post performance bonds of $2.5 million. One of Birmingham's most high profile moves – one that came three months before they opened their season – was signing Ken Stabler to a five-year, $850,000 contract that would make him the Americans signal caller in 1976. The former Alabama quarterback was at the top of his professional game with the Oakland Raiders, and he would join several other big names (including L.C. Greenwood of Pittsburgh and Bob Kuechenberg of Miami) in bolting the NFL for the Ams. But Stabler sued to get out of his contract (the story broke on the day the Americans won the World Bowl), knowing it would likely never be honored, and the influx of NFL superstars to the Magic City never materialized. In fact, the Birmingham Americans – for all practical purposes – ceased to exist just moments after defeating Florida at Legion Field.

Officially their demise came in January, 1975, when new WFL commissioner Chris Hemmeter (who led the Hawaiians franchise ownership group in 1974) revoked the franchise due to the fact that it still owed more than $2 million to take care of unpaid bills, player salaries and taxes. One of the more humiliating aspects of the Americans' dissolution came in March, 1975, when the Internal Revenue Service announced that it would auction off the contracts of 59 Birmingham players in an effort to recover more than $200,000 in Social Security and unemployment taxes from the franchise.   Still, Hemmeter promised that Birmingham would get another team to occupy Legion Field in 1975. I was relieved to hear it, especially since I had my doubts that the WFL would ever play another game. The question, of course, was whether or not Birmingham's new team could or would win my heart. First loves are tough acts to follow.

WFL: THE SEQUEL

The second season of the World Football League was actually the first season of The New League, Inc. Yep ... according to the 1975 WFL media guide, the organization that would field 11 teams that summer was an entirely new entity, one called The New League Inc., d.b.a. (doing business as) the World Football League. Officially formed on April 15, 1975, it paid $10,000 for rights to the name and logo in an effort to create some continuity from the inaugural season, although much had changed from Year One. The new WFL also vowed to help pay off the debts of the original league, which was retroactively dubbed the "Football Creditors Payment Plan, Inc." New League Inc. pledged 1.5 percent of its gross revenues over the next 12 years.

Eleven franchises started the 1975 season; the Birmingham Vulcans, Charlotte Hornets, Chicago Winds, the Hawaiians, Jacksonville Express, Memphis Southmen, Philadelphia Bell, Portland Thunder, San Antonio Wings, Shreveport Steamer and Southern California Sun. Memphis, Philly, Hawaii and Southern Cal were holdovers from 1974, with the Southmen and

Bell debt-free from first season obligations and the Hawaiians and Sun able to pay off what they owed before joining The New League, Inc. under new and/or altered ownership. Charlotte and Shreveport were also back in action, while three WFL cities (Birmingham, Chicago and Portland) were kept in place but rebranded. San Antonio was the result of the Florida Blazers moving, and Jacksonville was an "expansion" team (although you could stretch a point and say the Express were a Sharks rebrand; that franchise folded after 14 games in 1974).

After owners spent money they didn't have a year earlier, the new WFL would not have that issue thanks to "The Hemmeter Plan." While it sounded like the title of a suspense thriller starring Charles Bronson and Jill Ireland, it was, in fact, designed to –according to the media guide – "revolutionize the industry of professional sports." Basically, the idea was to make as many of the team's costs as possible "variable." And when it came to players, the standard contract was based on each man on the team receiving one percent of the gate – guaranteed.

If owners wanted to spend more money on a "star" player, they would have to put money in escrow to cover it.

"Last year's problems have been well-defined and are certainly an embarrassment to me," Hemmeter wrote in the 1975 media guide. "Unfortunately, even though the new league is an entirely separate entity, we are paying for the problems created by others in 1974. But we are rapidly overcoming those problems. I think this is the league of the future. Our plan will allow the WFL to endure as a financial entity, and with increased financial stability exploit itself on the field where it belongs." While I started my WFL fandom knowing nothing (and caring nothing) about the finances of the sport, by 1975 I was getting kinda interested. And after reading through the plan, it seemed like a good idea to me. Then again, I was making only $5 per yard in my grass cutting business, so the bar to impress me was rather low.

The in-game rules were identical to those of 1974, although they ditched the cool mustard ball for a normal, run-of-the-mill pigskin. (There were experimental rules in used in preseason games: field goals kicked inside the 10- yard line were worth one point and those made between the 10 and 30 counted two points. All others were worth three. And on third down plays the defensive team had to have four down linemen in 3-point stances). The schedule of contests that counted was cut to 18 games, with a pair of exhibitions thrown in, and instead of Wednesday-Thursday games most contests were scheduled for Saturdays and Sundays. The regular season didn't start until the first weekend in August and the playoffs weren't set to begin until the week of Christmas. One innovation they planned was taken from minor league baseball – namely, a split season.

Birmingham, Charlotte, Jacksonville, Memphis and Philadelphia made up the East Division, while Chicago, Hawaii, Portland, San Antonio, Shreveport and Southern Cal comprised the West Division. Six of the 11 teams were to qualify for the playoffs; the summer and fall champions of the East, summer and fall champions of the West, and the team from each division with the best overall record (or next in line if the team with the best record is a seasonal division winner). The biggest news splash of the season was the arrival of Larry Csonka, Paul Warfield and Jim Kiick from the Dolphins to the Southmen. Bassett had signed the trio to a future contract in 1974, and they were far and away the biggest attractions the WFL had to offer. While other league owners made financial promises they couldn't keep, Bassett was a man of his word who paid his players and paid his bills. Unfortunately, the league had no TV contract. If the WFL was hoping to lure casual fans for its second season, it was out of luck. But, the WFL had survived, sort of, and I was prepared to jump back on the bandwagon to support Birmingham's second professional football team in as many seasons.

BIRMINGHAM VULCANS (1975)

You've heard the expression, "same church, different pew?" The Vulcans - officially born on March 7, 1975 - were basically the Americans under new ownership. Really, that's exactly what they were. "The Birmingham Vulcans is everything we could've hoped for in a name for our new team," said Gotta who - at the time - was still head coach and general manager. "It personifies strength and civic pride." While Putnam was gone, local business leaders, led by Ferd Weil and A. E. Burgess, brought a new WFL franchise to the Magic City and it looked a whole lot like the old one. Gotta ultimately decided to give up the coaching reigns in order to become general manager, and Marvin Bass - who was an assistant to Gotta with the Ams - took over as head coach. Bass had 33 years' experience as a coach, including head coach at the University of South Carolina.

Gotta opted to concentrate solely on the GM role in his second year in Birmingham. "The availability of a fine coach like Marvin Bass made the decision easy for me," Gotta told United Press International. "I'm not worried about what happens on the field if I can give him the players."

But the best part, at least for me, was that Reed had the quarterbacking job all to himself after Mira had moved to Jacksonville to take charge of the Express offense. Several other players who had suited up the year before in Birmingham were back on the team, including Homan, Profit, Bishop, Cantrelle, Willingham and defensive standout Warren Capone. The biggest addition to the roster was Johnny Musso, the former University of Alabama great who had spent the previous three seasons with the CFL's British Columbia Lions. In 1973 he rushed for 1,029 yards and scored 10 touchdowns for BC, but played only three games in 1974 and had a pair of knee operations. Still, he said he was ready to "come home" and contribute. "I'm running at full speed and taking cuts," Musso told the Associated Press. "My leg is coming along fine. I'll find out real quick when I get to camp and take some licks."

The team's uniforms were almost identical except for the logo, which I still think is pretty cool. I'll always have a soft spot for the red, white and blue "A," but the stylish blue "V" wrapped around a football and holding a flame was enough to make me race to Pizitz (the major regional department store in Birmingham and Alabama) and grab a Vulcans-branded shirt. And in a way, this was "my" team in a literal sense; Vulcans stock was public and Pop bought $50 worth, which came with a certificate and a metal button that read, "I Own A Piece Of The Vulcans." And since Pop gave me the button, that meant

I owned a piece of the Vulcans because wearing a button is nine-tenths of the law, or something to that effect. In any case, it was a point of pride and all the more reason to once again give my heart and soul to Birmingham's WFL team.

PRESEASON

The first game I attended that season was actually a controlled scrimmage against Memphis on Thursday, July 3. A crowd of more than 30,000 were in steamy Legion Field that night – I assume many were interested in getting their first look at Csonka, Warfield and Kiick, as well as having a chance to cheer on Musso, a hometown hero who prepped at Banks High School in Birmingham. I wanted to see them, too, but I was more interested in checking out the Vulcans and getting an idea of how much of the WFL champion Ams they had in them.

And I was especially anxious to see "Rip" Reed go wire-to wire behind center. While I appreciated Mira and what he had done the year before, Reed was the QB of Birmingham's future – especially with Stabler out of the picture. I didn't realize the significance of having an African-American quarterback ... to me people were people, players were players, and the only colors I obsessed over were the ones worn by the teams. Reed had been a crowd favorite coming off the bench in 1974, and I never talked to, interacted with, or heard of a fan that wasn't thrilled he was going to be the leader of the

Vulcans. But Birmingham was a lightning rod of the civil rights movement, especially in the 1960s. Its reputation was marred by the bombing of 16th Street Baptist Church (which resulted in the deaths of four young African-American girls), and the racist regime of Birmingham Commissioner of Public Safety Eugene "Bull" Connor, who directed the use of attack dogs and fire hoses against civil rights activists. Less than a decade later, though, a city that – to many – was defined by segregation was embracing a black quarterback playing for a team that was a textbook example of integration. Legion Field, in fact, had never hosted a football team that was fully integrated until Southern California came to town on September 12, 1970, and beat Alabama, 42-21.

Perhaps if I had been a few years older I would've better appreciated the meaning of it all. Instead, I just knew that Reed was my favorite player (Jenkins, my 1974 hero, bolted to the NFL in 1975 and began a fine nine-year career with the Atlanta Falcons). Since the game against Memphis was basically just a glorified practice (no kickoffs, no punt returns, no QB blitzes), there was no reason to get overly excited or especially concerned about what happened. For the record, Birmingham won, 23-18, with Musso scoring the first touchdown for the Vulcans and generating the most noise from the crowd. Reed quarterbacked the first two quarters but reserves took over on both sides in the second half. Duron, another holdover from the Ams, worked the final 30 minutes and set himself up as Reed's backup for the 1975 season.   "I didn't know how to approach this scrimmage," Bass said. "It's so rewarding to see an organization that had the things which happened to us last year come back and get off to such a wonderful start this year."

Nine days later I was back at Legion Field with a posse of high school friends (and 18,500 fans total) as Birmingham hosted Portland. The Vulcans won, 25-9 (that was one of the exhibitions that featured, one, two and three-point field goals and each team kicked one two-point field goal) but what I remember more than anything is that one of my friend's dad dropped us off at the game and picked us up when it was over. I had never been to Legion Field without adult supervision and let me tell you, it was liberating. I think I might have even cussed – although I made sure to do it out of earshot of any adult in the stadium. I mean, parents have spies everywhere. A week later Birmingham went to Shreveport and nipped the Steamer, 31-30, to close out its exhibition slate.

EARLY STRUGGLES

Opening night for the Vulcans was August 2, when Abe Gibron's Winds came to town. The attendance plan was iffy because Don and his wife were expecting their first child, so we were going to make sure the little fellow stayed in the oven before buying tickets. He did not. My oldest nephew has the honor of sharing a birthday with the first regular season day of the Vulcans, one that I ended up spending at home so I could listen to the game on the radio. (To prove I still had priorities, I did go by the hospital to visit the newest addition to the Adamson tribe. Like most babies hailing from our family, he looked like a smaller and very pink version of Winston Churchill). Anyway, it was just as well that I happened to miss this game because Namath wasn't behind center for Chicago.

With the blessings of Hemmeter and the rest of the WFL owners, the Winds went after Broadway Joe, making every effort to lure him to the Windy City and give Chicago the ultimate marquee player. (That effort, by the way, was an offer of $4 million). But he wisely declined, leaving Pete Beathard to run the show. Oh, if you were a fan of defense it was a great game, I suppose; the teams combined for just 10 points. Birmingham got all 10 (all coming in the first half) and launched the new franchise and new league with a 10-0 victory in front of a little over 28,000 fans. Reed had to exit the game with a hip-pointer in the second quarter, which contributed to the Vulcans' offensive woes. "Our defense shut them out, and that's as good as you can get," Bass told the Anniston Star. "I don't think we were as sharp offensively as we've been in some of our past games. When we lost Matthew Reed, it sure didn't help any. Matthew's a threat any time he's in the game and that caused us to lose some continuity."

The low turnout showed that fans – even the rabid fans Birmingham was famous for – were skeptical about the "comeback." The next week, a 23-17 win over Philadelphia at the Gray Lady, was watched by only

21,000. This was another game that I missed because I went to a party that night. And while I don't remember whose party it was, I was a future freshman at Huffman High School, so I'm sure it was epic and much more important than professional football. Week three resulted in a 22-11 loss to Jacksonville in the Gator Bowl, at tilt that saw Mira, now running the Express offense, manage a solid game. But it was Reamon, the former Blazer, who hurt Birmingham the most with a strong night running. That was another game I watched via the miracle of cable television. And while the result was disappointing for us stockholders, it was a long season, and Birmingham had never lost a WFL game at Legion Field. That being the case, I felt really confident about the August 23 home game against Southern Cal, one that I would attend in person with Don, Dave and a date.

I'd saved up enough grass-cutting cash to bring a "plus one," a young woman I'll call Theresa (because her name is Theresa), and one who was a gifted softball player and sports fan. And I figured this was a great game to attend because the new-look Sun featured three former USC greats – Anthony Davis, Pat Haden and J.K. McKay. I had watched all three in college, and was genuinely excited about seeing them play at the next level.

A crowd of about 30,000 dotted Legion Field that night, and for the first time I can remember our seats were not on the upper deck side. We were down low near the 30 yard line, though, so they were plenty good. I guess I should've known the evening would not go as I hoped just a few minutes before game time, when I bought two hot dogs and two cokes from a stadium hawker. After I took a healthy bite of my pregame meal, Theresa asked me a question. Now, someone more polished in the dating game would've finished chewing before answering. Not me. Instead, I tried to do both, which resulted in a small, damp chunk of bun flying out of my mouth and hitting her left forearm. I was mortified. To her credit, she deftly swatted the offending bun part away without comment, but she knew I had done it and I knew she knew I had done it, and I spent the rest of the night playing from behind, so to speak.

As for the game, it was quite entertaining if you didn't have a dog in the fight. After the Sun grabbed a 7-3 lead in the first quarter, the teams combined for 36 points in the second frame, with the Vulcans scoring 22 and taking a 25-21 lead into the locker room. But it was all Southern Cal the rest of the way, offensively and defensively. Reed, struggling with the injury suffered a week earlier, didn't start and failed to complete a pass when he came into the game late. Duron hit eight of 22 aerials but was intercepted twice. After the Sun took a 28-25 lead with a third quarter touchdown, Haden sealed the deal in the fourth when he connected with Keith Denson on a 35-yard scoring play to make it 35-25. That's how it ended, and that was also the end of Birmingham's perfect WFL record in Birmingham. What's worse, the Vulcans' 1975 worksheet dropped to 2-2, making them look like anything but champions. Oh, and Theresa's and my relationship never fully recovered from the hot dog incident. Flying bun chunks have a tendency to tear couples apart.

TROUBLE BREWING

The good news, at least for the Vulcans, is that they bounced back the following Saturday with a 21-8 win over Shreveport at Legion Field. The bad news is that less than 20,000 paying customers showed up to see it, and attendance was bad all across the league. On Sept. 2, the Winds were kicked out of the league after a pair of investors pulled their money, preventing the franchise from adhering to the Hemmeter Plan. "We agreed from Day One that kind of violation would not be tolerated," Hemmeter told the Associated Press. And considering the team had drawn less than 4,000 to its lone game at Soldier Field and didn't even have a radio contract, this was more or less a mercy killing. League officials tried to put a positive spin on it, saying that getting rid of the one weak link would make the chain stronger. I didn't buy it.

"It was a singular case," Hemmeter said. "From a business standpoint, it is certainly a more responsible act to shut down a potential problem than to allow the potential for future problems to exist. We are not willing to gamble of the future of the league." After I read about the Winds' demise in the paper, I remember asking Pop what he thought it meant for the rest of the league. "I'm afraid it means this the last year of the WFL," he said. "They don't have a TV contract and I just don't think enough people are interested." He was right. In fact, the game against Southern Cal – the flying bun chunk game – was the last one I ever attended.

OCTOBER DEMISE

Although I promised myself I wouldn't jump off the Birmingham bandwagon again after the Americans won the World Bowl, I kinda did. The Vulcans followed up their back-to-back losses with a four-game winning streak – beating Shreveport 21-8, Portland 26-8, San Antonio 33-24, and Charlotte, 22-16 – but my interest was confined to following them loosely on the radio. I'm sure I had several chances to return to Legion Field and watch them, but for me, it was almost like seeing an old friend waste away. Almost every day there were reports in the newspapers that the WFL was on its last legs, and I was now aware enough to realize it would take a miracle to save the league. I didn't have faith that a miracle was forthcoming. The Vulcans lost their second game of the season to Jacksonville, 26-18, on September 27, but stood at 7-3 with the summer season of the split schedule complete. They finished a half game behind East Division leader Memphis (7-2), so they needed to either win the fall season or have the best overall record in the East to assure a playoff spot. Fortunately, Birmingham had a chance to get the fall season off to a great start with back-to-back games against the Southmen, and this mini-series reignited my interest.

I spent Sunday, October 12, listening to the game with Pop.

Birmingham came away with an 18-14 victory at the Liberty Bowl, with all of the Vulcans' points coming in the second half.

It appeared Memphis was going to win when Marshall – who was key in the Southmen's big victory over the Americans a year earlier – apparently caught a TD pass from White on a fourth-and-13 play with time winding down. But officials huddled and ruled the pass incomplete, infuriating the 20,000-plus partisans and allowing Birmingham to take over on downs and run out the clock. "This was the greatest and most exciting game I've ever seen," Bass told the Courier News of Blytheville, Arkansas. "There wasn't a dull moment in it. Tonight surpasses anything I've ever been associated with." A week later the old rivals would play at Legion Field, and I thought seriously about going. But ... I had already decided to spend my money on the Alabama-Tennessee game at Legion Field played the day before (a 30-7 Crimson Tide victory), so that left me with an embarrassment of funds on October 19. I ended up listening to the game at a friend's house. When it was done, Birmingham dominated to the tune of 21-0, with the defense registering six sacks and the offense getting all it needed off a Reed-to-Duron TD pass, and scoring runs by Cantrelle and Musso. "I wanted this game badly, because it's a crucial time as everyone knows," Bass told the Montgomery Advertiser. "And we wanted a real spectator show for our fans. We may lose some football games down the road, but I still think we're a great football team." Roughly 35,000 fans watched the clash, which was by far the largest crowd of the season and gave Birmingham a league-best 9-3 record. "Our offense was slow getting started," Bass told the Associated Press. "But our defense did a super job, and that was the story. Any time you hold Memphis scoreless, somebody is playing football." Those in attendance have the honor of witnessing the last WFL game to be played in the Magic City. I wish now I had been among them.

WORLD FAILURE LEAGUE

The WFL folded on Wednesday, October 22, with owners voting 6-4 to close up shop due to a tidal wave of red ink and lack of interest from ticket-buying customers. Average per game attendance was down to 13,325, and it had dropped each weekend. Philadelphia drew only 3,705 fans per game and Portland's last home contest – a 28-25 victory over San Antonio – marked its lowest turnout ever when only 3,818 people showed up at Civic Stadium. The ownership groups in Memphis, Charlotte, Jacksonville and San Antonio voted to play out the rest of the season, but when they were outnumbered, the league officially died. "Our decision not to proceed is due primarily to our collective inability to penetrate markets in WFL franchise cities," Hemmeter told the Associated Press. "We came to the realization that the ability of the WFL to penetrate its markets to the extent necessary to make the WFL a success would most likely require two or three more years of operation with capital requirements of $25 million to $40 million." The WFL left behind the greatest financial disaster in professional sports history and hundreds of football players, coaches and staff members were left looking for jobs. The league that began with such high hopes reached its ultimate low point.

"No way I'm staying around," Reed told the Associated Press as he cleaned out his locker on the WFL's final day of existence. "I'm leaving tonight ... going home where I belong. I'm going home to rest." Reed said he knew the end was near with each passing weekend. "I wasn't surprised," he said. "I just didn't know when it was going to happen. This has been a really enjoyable season, I'll have to say that." Vulcans' defensive end Jim McKinney – formerly of the Dallas Cowboys – told the Associated Press he thought Birmingham was good enough to compete in the NFL. "I guarantee this team could compete with any team we played against while I was at Dallas," he said. "I've only been here eight weeks, but this is a good football team."

I heard the news that night and was sad about it, but not devastated. I was certainly not surprised. I guess I had grown up a lot since that snowy night when I found out the World Football League was headed for Birmingham. In just two and half seasons (and my transition from grammar school to high school), I came to realize that sometimes games are businesses and sometimes businesses, well, go out of business. I often wonder if signing Namath would've made a difference.

The guy was credited with giving the AFL "legitimacy" by leading the Jets to victory in Super Bowl III, but I'm not sure he could've done anything beyond maybe – maybe – helping the WFL complete its 1975 season. That's probably wishful thinking, too, considering Csonka, Kiick and Warfield couldn't save it. Back in 2004 I interviewed Namath for a story during Iron Bowl week, and I had to ask him about the WFL deal that never was. He laughed and said "Yeah, I thought about it, and that was a lot of money, but the way the WFL was going I just didn't think jumping leagues was the right thing to do at the time."

Birmingham and Memphis applied for membership in the NFL for 1976, but there was no way they were going to absorbed. Seattle and Tampa Bay had already been granted expansion franchises for that year, and the NFL had the luxury of picking and choosing its owners and cities. They weren't about to take two clubs from a failed league – especially one that had raided it for players and forced owners to pay out more money to ensure that their stars wouldn't jump. NFL Commissioner Pete Rozelle effectively ruled out Birmingham and Memphis on Dec. 17, 1975, saying expansion teams must clear three hurdles to be considered. "The first hurdle is the state of mind," Rozelle told the Associated Press, referring to the economy. "And then selection of cities and ownership in those cities. It's safe to say Memphis and Birmingham did not clear that first big hurdle.

"Sports leagues have folded and contracted, teams have folded and other leagues have abandoned expansion plans. This, plus litigation that we're not involved in, has created a cloud of uncertainty among league owners."

Over the last 40-plus years, I've created a shrine to the league that serves as the centerpiece of my "Fan Cave." I have official WFL balls, dozens of programs – even media guides from all 12 of the original franchises. I started collecting mini helmets in the early 2000s, and I have one display that features helmets representing all the teams that played in 1974, even the ones that moved during the course of the season. Call it an obsession if you like – I won't argue the point. But I miss the WFL, and especially the Americans and Vulcans. I wish they'd had more time, and that I had spent more time visiting them at their big house on Graymont Avenue.

AMERICAN FOOTBALL ASSOCIATION

If you've never heard of the AFA, you're not alone. Only real football diehards remember the league that lasted from 1977 to 1983, leaving a legacy of decent football that went virtually unnoticed. While you can't swing a helmet without hitting a semi-pro league, the AFA was different in that players were actually paid – not much, but a little. I always shake my head when I hear about a "semi-pro" team, because that's just a way for amateur teams to make themselves feel better. You have to wonder, though, if the money AFA players made was worth the damage to their bodies. League officials called their pay scale the "AFA Plan of Organization," but it was really the "Hemmeter Plan" under a different name; travel, rent, etc. was paid for through escrow accounts, while each player pocketed one percent of the gate. Considering the gates were often terrible, compensation barely rose above pocket change.

The inaugural campaign was Texas heavy, made up of the Austin Texans, Fort Worth Stars, Houston Seagulls, Oklahoma City Warriors, San Antonio Charros and Wichita Falls Steelers.

Harry Lander, one of the league's founders and head coach of the Charros, had big plans for the little league. His previous pro football claim to fame was a brief stint as partner of the WFL Wings. "Next year our objective is to go back to Birmingham, Memphis, Jacksonville, Arkansas, Oklahoma, Kentucky, Tennessee and Mississippi and form a Southeast Division," he told the San Antonio Express. "Then we will have New Mexico, Arizona, Nevada, Southern California and Utah in the Western Division. A regional concept in areas that don't have NFL football – that's what we're after." The second season, 1978, featured a Western Division that was, in fact, the California Football League. Its teams – the Fairfield Flyers, Long Beach Mustangs, Los Angeles Norsemen, Sacramento Buffaloes, San Gabriel Saints, San Jose Tigers, Southern California Rhinos, and Twin City Cougars – played amongst themselves and the only game against actual AFA teams came in the championship game.

The commissioner of the AFA that season was a lawyer named Payne Roye, who tried to market the league as the next best thing to the National Football League. "From the standpoint of quality, we're less than the NFL and better than the top college programs," he told the Clarion-Ledger of Jackson, Mississippi, for a December, 1978 story. "It's the best besides the NFL. "We have top-notch teams ready to go. I feel we're filling a void that's existed for some time for entertainment on Saturday night. We're filling a void that exists between the NFL and college level."

In 1979, the year of the Vulcans, the league had nine teams divided into two divisions: Alabama, the Arkansas Champs, Carolina Chargers, Jacksonville Firebirds, Kentucky Trackers, Mississippi Stars, San Antonio Charros, Shreveport Steamer, and Tulsa Mustangs. In 1980 there were eight teams: Carolina, Jacksonville, Kentucky, and West Virginia (Rockets) in the East and Austin (Texans), Fort Worth (Wranglers), San Antonio and Shreveport in the West. San Antonio and Shreveport were the only franchises from 1978 that returned the following season. The league had a series of commissioners, including former NFL quarterback Billy Kilmer. He guided the AFA in 1981 (he previously coached the Shreveport team in 1979), but he worked without pay during his tenure as league boss and quit after one year in charge. By 1982 there were 18 teams across three divisions: Alabama, the Austin Texans, Buffalo Geminis, Canton Bulldogs, Carolina Storm, Florida Sun, Georgia Pride, Houston Armadillos, Jacksonville Sunbirds, Oklahoma Thunder, Racine Gladiators, Roanoke Express, San Antonio Bulls, Shreveport Americans, Tallahassee Statesmen, Texas Wranglers, Virginia Chargers, and West Virginia Rockets. That was the season the league was supposed to step up and prove itself as a quality minor league. "It's a proven fact football is the No. 1 spectator sport," AFA commissioner Roger Gill told the Milwaukee Sentinel for an April 3, 1982, story on the league. "What we've done is taken football at the start of fan interest in June and end it before the start of pro and college ball. We think we have the ideal situation. We play on summer evenings in shirtsleeve weather, which is perfect from a spectator standpoint. There's really a void at that time. All you've got is submarine races and baseball."

ALABAMA VULCANS (1979)

By the time this incarnation of the Vulcans came to town, I was a big boy – wrapping up my senior year in high school and prepping to begin my first year at the University of Alabama in Birmingham. My sports horizons had also broadened since 1975 – quite dramatically, actually. I had become passionate about both soccer and hockey, with the North American Soccer League sparking my love for real world "football," and the World Hockey Association – and especially the Birmingham Bulls – helping me evolve into a diehard fan of the fastest collision game on ice. While my bedroom walls were once decorated with Americans and Vulcans pennants (I even had a Charlotte Hornets pennant, for some reason), they were now placed in storage and replaced by soccer and hockey tributes. Posters of Pele and Kyle Rote Jr. shared billing with Birmingham Bulls, Atlanta Flames and New York Rangers pennants. My love for football was still there, of course, but from a professional standpoint, it was still mostly confined to the Jets and Rams. I realized that Legion Field would never be home to an NFL team and the WFL was probably as close as we'd ever come to the big time. So, when I read that that Birmingham had been granted a franchise in something known as the American Football Association, I was only mildly interested.

The WFL tried and failed at major league football, so there was no reason to believe a lesser gridiron product had a legitimate chance to survive. And three months before the AFA team came to town Burgess, an official with the WFL Vulcans, said he would not be involved in this league. "Anything less than the best is not going to go over in Birmingham," Burgess told the Birmingham News. "Therefore, I indicated to those people when they contacted me about a month ago that I have no interest in their operation." Still, they were coming to town, so what the heck – why not give 'em a shot? Hockey season was still several months away and there were worse ways to spend a summer night. Obviously, there was nothing close to a media frenzy during the lead-up to their season opener, but Lander, serving as team owner and head coach, had been successful with two other teams in the AFA (San Antonio and Shreveport) and said he was coming to Birmingham to make the Vulcans the "bell cow" of the league. "This is my fourth time to go through something like this with a virgin franchise," Lander told the Montgomery Advertiser. "We're by no means a semi-pro operation. It's ridiculous to say that the only good football players are in the NFL. Our American colleges are turning out 8,000 senior football players a year and only about 100 of them are making it in the NFL."

Lander hoped to stock his team with a lot of players with local ties, although there were very few who would be considered former college superstars. The AFA had no draft but there was something of an informal agreement among teams that any player who graduated from a college in a particular state became property of the AFA team in that state. "We'll have an outstanding brand of football," Lander told the Atlanta Constitution. "Once you get past the real superstars in the NFL, the next 1,000 players are pretty much the same. We'll sign players released by the NFL and players who aren't even drafted." Starting quarterback Chris Vacarella, for example, was a backup QB at Auburn in 1973 and 1974, but spent his final two seasons on The Plain playing running back and wide receiver. Lander also tried to spin the narrative that the AFA wasn't minor league at all, and was on par with the CFL. (It was, and it wasn't). There were some "name" players on the original roster, though. Offensive linemen Dave Ostrowski (Auburn) and Lou Green (Alabama) were well-known to area college football fans, as was fullback Kenny Burks (Auburn). The Vulcans opened the season on May 19 against the Carolina Chargers at Legion Field, so a high school buddy and I decided to check it out.

The main draw for me, as silly as it sounds, was the home team's colors and logo; they wore black, red and silver, and sported a badge that incorporated both the Americans' and 1975 Vulcans' logo. It was clever and cool and football fashion has always been important to me. Sadly, the team was not dressed for success on opening night. Oh, they won the game – 28-0 – with Vacarella hitting James Coleman (a Jacksonville State product) for a pair of touchdowns and Alabama clearly looking like the better side. But their helmet logos weren't ready, nor were their dark home jerseys, and they looked like a team getting ready to play a closed scrimmage instead of one competing in a season opener. It was not a great first impression, and the fact that 4,200 fans showed up (Lander said during the week of the game he was expecting 20,000) told me that the magic of the beloved WFL was nowhere to be found in this league. This team might've incorporated the old nicknames, but there was nothing remotely reminiscent about the "good old days." An even bigger issue was ticket prices; I wasn't thrilled about paying $7 to watch minor league football. That was just a dollar less than the Americans and original Vulcans charged. Don't get me wrong – I couldn't hold the jockstrap of any guy on the field – but those were major league prices for a product that clearly wasn't major league. I went to one other game that season – I can't even recall which game it was or whether or not Alabama won – and remember the team and 1979 AFA more for what happened off the field than on it.

The Tulsa Mustangs "withdrew" five games into the season and the league responded by dropping from two divisions to one, canning the split season format and changing the numbers of wins and losses for seven of eight teams. The reasons for the altered records were so bizarre it gave me a headache trying to figure it out. It had something to do with too many teams having open dates or some such nonsense. "We've got a good thing going, everything is fine, then you come up with this bush-league stuff," Charros personnel director Jerry Wilson told The Times of Shreveport. "It's something you'd expect out of a Pop Warner group. It's Little League – a joke, a real joke." On the field – for a time at least – Alabama appeared to be the class of the league. Following the opening night win over Carolina, Lander's team beat Tulsa (18-0), Mississippi (14-3), Jacksonville (48-0), and Arkansas (49-14). A road loss at Kentucky (28-14) was followed by victories over Mississippi (20-14), Kentucky (27-0), Shreveport (20-17), Jacksonville (17-14) and Shreveport again (13-7), putting the record at 10-1. But then came a loss to San Antonio (21-12), wins over Mississippi (17-0) and Arkansas (38-0), setbacks to Jacksonville (27-26) and San Antonio (17-10), a victory against Kentucky (41-6) and a regular season-ending thrashing at the hands of Carolina (52-14).

The only national attention the Vulcans (and league) received was when Alabama signed former Pittsburgh Steelers quarterback Joe Gilliam, who made news by borrowing Lander's car and disappearing for a few days. Gilliam never played a down for Birmingham, and the team itself finished 13-5, losing to Jacksonville, 28-21, in the first round of the playoffs. Oh, and one game the Vulcans had to loan the Arkansas team both uniforms and half a dozen players; the Champs were short on both when they got to Legion Field. That was some pretty bush-league stuff right there. I have no recollection of when the team officially folded (although it obviously did, because it wasn't back in 1980), and had lost any and all interest by the time it reached the finish line.

ALABAMA MAGIC (1982)

Most of us have seminal moments that define us as human beings, and mine came in the spring of 1982 when I received a call from officials with Deep South Sports Projects, Inc. They let me know that I had won the "Name the Team" contest for their Birmingham entry in the AFA. Hey ... that's heady stuff when you're a 21-year old. In reality, it was no more significant than being the fifth caller on a local radio show and winning a two-night stay at a hotel in Gadsden. It was a mere burp in the buffet of life, and barely a footnote in the history of Birmingham pro football. Still, it happened, and I'd be a fool to deny my place in history. I had submitted several nicknames for the contest, including Magicians (my hopeful name for our WFL franchise), Yellowhammers and Ironmen, but they selected "Magic," which I assume was the nickname at the top of my list.

And in order to make the whole state get behind the club, it would be called the "Alabama Magic." (One of the reasons I chose Magic was because I lived in the Magic City and assumed the team would represent Birmingham. By calling the team "Alabama," it made the nickname less meaningful. Perhaps they should've selected "Yellowhammers").

There were others who chose that nickname as well, but mine was the name drawn from a hat, so that makes me the winner and you can never take that away from me. What did I win? Thanks for asking. There were four tickets to each Alabama Magic home game (three games were played at Legion Field, one in Anniston and one scheduled in Selma but never played); a team jersey (a white half-jersey with the number 50); a lifetime membership to Singles nightclub (which I never used because while I was certainly single at the time, disco sucked); a $15 gift certificate to an office supplies store (I can't remember the name of the store, I just know they sold office supplies and I bought $15 worth of them) and a case of eggs. The case of eggs (15 dozen) seemed like an odd prize when compared to the others, but I wasn't complaining. I picked them up at the team's headquarters (an old house that seemed to be out in the middle of nowhere), and carefully loaded them in my car. The transaction was how I assumed a drug deal would go down, only without guns and with dairy products. They were delicious, by the way, although I assume they might've been the catalyst to my high cholesterol issues later in life. Really, I entered the contest just for kicks and giggles, never expecting to win and having no real interest in the league or team. After all, I had been down the AFA road before and as much as the folks wanted people to take the league seriously, it was a hard sell.

That being said, the team did hold a hybrid news conference/banquet at a hotel to introduce the team with "a Magical future," and former American Football League player Charlie Hennigan (who was the Shreveport Americans' coach/general manager in 1982 ... at least for the first game) was the featured speaker.

Talking to him was a real treat for me because of my love for the AFL, and I was able to eat without having to pay for it. That put the night in the "W" column. A few weeks later the team unveiled its logo which, sadly, was a letdown to me. It was a wonky blue star on top of the letters "A" and "M" and outlined in bold red. The next day the Birmingham News ran a story about the newly christened Alabama Magic, and even mentioned my name. Almost. One line in the article read, "The winner of the name-the-team contest was Scott Johnson." I briefly thought about having my last name legally changed so there would never be any confusion as to who the winner actually was, but I settled for writing a letter to the editor that set the record straight. I felt future generations deserved to know the truth.

Anyway, the team was also part of my early journalism resume because I interviewed Magic quarterback Mark Cahill for a story in the UAB Kaleidoscope newspaper, where I served as sports editor. Cahill was Steve Bartkowski's backup at California in 1974 before quitting the team and transferring to UNLV, but had become a semi-pro football star for the Greater Northwest Football Association a year later while guiding the fortunes of the

Pierce County Bengals. In fact, he was 1975 Player of the Year in the league, and seven years later was still trying to make his way in professional football. In 1981, while playing for the AFA's San Antonio Charros, he threw for 31 touchdowns and was named to the circuit's All-Star team. He seemed like a good dude, and stressed the fact that there were a lot of quality football players outside the NFL and CFL. He also understood why Birmingham fans might have a hard time accepting the new team. "The old Americans and Vulcans drew well, then (the WFL) got into trouble and folded," Cahill said. "The previous AFA team (in Birmingham) had poor management and they went under. The people here have just been burned too many times, and they're sort of reluctant to support another football team. We have some excellent players and franchises in this league." This AFA, he said, was a player's best option if he wanted to stay in the game and one day make some money playing it.

In terms of name recognition, the roster headliner was former Auburn QB Charlie Trotman, who would be used more as a running back and wide receiver with Birmingham's AFA team. "I wouldn't be playing at all if I didn't think I had a chance of getting on with an NFL team, a Canadian team or the USFL next year," Trotman told the Montgomery Advertiser. "I just don't feel I've had a legitimate shot at making it yet." On opening day, the team had signed seven former Auburn and three ex-Alabama players (including Tide defensive back Tyrone King and Tiger Phil Gargis). I went to the

May 29 opener with Pop – and unlike many trips I had made to see the WFL and college games, traffic in and around Legion Field was no issue. We parked in a lot just a few feet from one of the gates, and as we were preparing to go in, there was a guy – I kid you not – trying to scalp tickets. They were $8 face value, which is a price I wouldn't have paid. I couldn't imagine anyone asking for more. As he haggled with a man and his young son, I pulled two out of my wallet (remember ... I had four tickets to each home game) and handed them to the duo. They were about 40 rows up and near the 50-yard line – right next to us (obviously) and pretty good seats. "They're free," I said, and Pop chuckled as the would-be scalper gave me a death stare as we headed to our choice spots on the aluminum bleachers.

As for the game, the Magic pulled off a 37-32 victory over the Jacksonville Sunbirds, a fun affair played before just under 2,000 fans. Cahill threw four touchdown passes and fans got to see a blast from the WFL past when former Birmingham Vulcans kicker Ron Slovensky handled the Magic's PAT duties. I also wrote about the experience for the Kaleidoscope, giving the contest high marks for entertainment (lots of scoring and a few big plays), but noting the extreme shortage of fannies plopped on the bleachers. I realize number of fans has nothing to do with level of play, but number of fans has everything to do with how long a team gets before it's leveled by the Grim Reaper. Perhaps that article was part of a self-fulfilling prophecy, because I never attended another game. "They could save a lot of

money playing at Lawson Field," said Pop, referring to
the 7,500-seat high school stadium used by Birmingham
high schools. "Playing in front of all these empty seats
just looks silly. Plus, I bet the rent at Lawson Field is a
lot cheaper."

Like their AFA predecessors back in 1979, the
football was decent; I guess using minor league baseball
terms, it was AA caliber, with some teams flirting with
AAA talent. "The quality of football is not all that bad,"
Trotman told the Montgomery Advertiser early in the
1982 season. "We couldn't beat an NFL team, but the
teams that make the AFA finals could play with most any
college team." Regardless, I just couldn't make myself
drive to Legion Field (or any other of the designated
home sites) and watch another team stocked by players I
was largely unfamiliar with in another league that I knew
was headed to the scrapheap. Plus, 70,000 empty seats
does not make for a terrific atmosphere. Besides,
Birmingham had been awarded a franchise in the new
United States Football League, which was set to begin
play in 1983. For the first time since the days of the WFL,
the USFL had me excited about pro football returning
to the Magic City.

As a postscript it should be noted that the Magic –
like the Alabama Vulcans – was a one and done team.
They started 6-1, following up the Jacksonville win with
33-0 and 28-0 wins over Florida and Tallahassee,
respectively, then a 29-13 loss to Carolina. Alabama then
beat Georgia (17-16), Jacksonville (37-9) and Florida (a
2-0 win by forfeit; the Panama City-based franchise

folded midseason) before closing out with three losses – 19-14 to Tallahassee, 17-14 to Carolina and 16-14 to Georgia. A 6-4 record wasn't good enough to make the playoffs, and then the Magic vanished. Head coach Steve Patton was only 29 years old, but did a good enough job to parlay his one-year stay in Birmingham into a solid career with a whistle and clipboard. In 1983 he led the Carolina Storm to the AFA title, while also earning the league's Coach of the Year honors. He had college coaching stints at three different schools, earning Coach of the Year accolades once at Mars Hill and twice while at Gardner-Webb. And in 1985, he was named Division II National Coach of the Year.

I wish I still had some mementos from the Magic's one not-so-magical season, but except for a program, I don't. The eggs went quickly and a dog chewed up my jersey. I think it was a dog ... it could've been a really large rat, I suppose. It was a long time ago and really makes no difference now.

RIP, AFA

None of the league's teams ever became box office successes, and if a franchise lasted more than one season, that was a major accomplishment. And there was no TV deal other than local stations occasionally broadcasting games; without that, the league had no chance at long-term survival. Having never seen a Continental Football League or Atlantic Coast Football League game – well respected minor leagues that came before it – I have no idea how the AFA compared in the level-of-play department. Regardless, semi-pro outdoor football (or even $100 a game outdoor football) isn't built to last. Baseball, hockey and now basketball have thriving farm systems, but college football is the only developmental circuit that has ever lasted.

The final year of the AFA was 1983, which was also the first season of the United States Football League. Gill, who by 1983 had gone from league commissioner to head coach of the San Antonio Bulls, already announced he'd be joining San Antonio's USFL entry in 1984 as general manager. "I would venture to say this will be the last year for the AFA," he told the Austin-American Statesman. "San Antonio has furnished a lot of leadership in the past to keep the league going, and that leadership may be lacking. Pro football is virtually a year-round operation now and the USFL will be operating at the same time of year as the AFA." The Carolina Storm and Canton Bulldogs were set to be members of the International Football League in 1984. In fact, legendary NFL quarterback Roman Gabriel was named the Storm's head coach, but the IFL - hoping to compete with the USFL during the spring - never got off the ground and, thus, the last vestiges of the AFA were gone.

UNITED STATES FOOTBALL LEAGUE

True story, at least as far as you know ... While taking an elective course at UAB back in 1980, one of my assignments was to do a short paper outlining a proposed business. My idea was for an American professional football league that started in April and ended with a championship game played on July 4.

I called it the North American Football League, and it would have teams in major markets across the United States and Canada. My two best gimmicks involved "Team USA" and "Team Canada," which would be a pair of franchises that played at different stadiums across their respective nations. That means if you didn't have an NAFL team in your city, you could claim ownership of the team that represented your country.

I was really proud of myself for coming up with that concept.

The reason this league had a chance at success was because it would not have to compete head-to-head with the NFL. And playing in football's "offseason" meant it would have access to big stadiums and, more importantly, fans who wouldn't have to worry about dividing their loyalties. It kinda sounds like I'm trying to take credit for the formation of the USFL, doesn't it? Wish I could, but I was many years late to the punch.

New Orleans businessman Dave Dixon had an idea for a league like this back in the mid-1960s, even as the NFL and AFL were battling it out for fans and players. In April, 1965, the Los Angeles Times reported that Dixon was seeking franchises for an eight-team league to begin play in 1966 featuring Anaheim, Atlanta, Los Angeles, Houston, Miami, New York, New Orleans and either San Francisco or Seattle. The season was to run from January through May. I promise, though, I knew nothing about Dixon when I wrote the paper. I bring it up only to show that the crazy idea of a spring/summer football league was never crazy at all, and many people had probably thought about it for many years. Fortunately, it was Dixon's thoughts that were put into action when the USFL became an actual thing on May 11, 1982. "Our league believes the sports fan in the United States wants to see more than the current 16-game professional football season," said Peter Spivak, the original USFL president, at the league's introductory news conference. "After all, his favorite baseball team plays 162 games and the basketball schedule runs 82 games." When you put it like that, it makes a lot of sense. Spivak said a study conducted by Frank N. Magid Associates, Inc., convinced everyone involved that a spring league was viable. "While the fans' reactions were initially negative when informed about the league's proposed schedule of March to July, this opinion

reversed itself when respondents were made aware of the
USFL's commitment to establishing a league built by
owners who possess a solid financial base and who are
recognized as people of outstanding personal
reputation," he said. After the news broke, I had a
spirited discussion about the league with Pop. He was
my best friend as well as my dad, and we could talk about
virtually any subject regardless of where we stood on the
issue. He liked to say we could "disagree without being
disagreeable," and we most certainly disagreed on the
USFL, at least in its infancy. "I just don't see how it's
going to last, not going up against baseball season," he
said. "People are used to watching baseball in the spring
and summer." Baseball was Pop's favorite sport; I'm not
sure he ever missed a televised Braves game. I, on the
other hand, liked baseball fine, but it had to share my fan
space with other sports. I certainly enjoyed going to
Rickwood Field and watching the Birmingham Barons
play, and I wasn't opposed to loading up the family
truckster and heading up I-20 to see Atlanta's National
League club on occasion. Yet I had already become
engrossed in the NASL, so baseball wasn't my No. 1
even before football. In fact, thanks to soccer, it was my
No. 2 in the spring and summer. And if I had the choice
of watching quality American football over baseball in
the spring and summer, football would win every time. I
said something to the effect of, "It may not last, but it
won't be because of baseball. Baseball games are every
day, and these games would be once or twice a week. I
think it has a chance."

By 1983, college basketball was my sport of choice, thanks to being a UAB student and thanks to Gene Bartow putting Blazer hoops on the map. I also still worked as s sports writer for the school paper, so it was the athletic events played by the college team that interested me most. I had fallen away from college football a bit since I was at UAB and – at the time – there were no Blazers to pull for on the gridiron. However, I had become a more serious fan of pro football. The Jets were back to being competitive (they made it to the AFC Championship Game in the strike-shortened 1982 season), and thanks to that work stoppage, I actually got to see a few CFL games on TV as well. That being the case, I could certainly find room for more professional football, and the brain trust of the USFL convinced me to buy in right from the outset. At the inaugural news conference, it was announced that the league would field 12 franchises in its first season in Birmingham, Boston, Chicago, Denver, Detroit, Los Angeles, New Jersey, Oakland, Philadelphia, Phoenix, Tampa Bay and Washington. "We're providing that other season for professional football," said Dixon, the founder as well as owner of the Chicago franchise.

Obviously hearing Birmingham was part of it was the headline for me, but knowing the league was hitting all the major markets was a sign that it was going big. More remarkable, especially for that era, was that the USFL had already secured a two-year television deal with both ABC and ESPN. That was huge. While the WFL had to settle for a syndicated network that local channels may or may not pick up, this was big league stuff; at the time ABC was the main outlet for college football, as well as the home of NFL Monday Night Football. ESPN, on the other hand, was still a young network but had upgraded tremendously from its days of showing tractor pulls and summer league basketball. ABC handled Sunday telecasts, and ESPN was set to show two primetime games per week.

It had 10 months to go from announcing its formation to playing its first game, and during that time it did just about everything to show it was determined to be a major football league. Its earthquake move came when it convinced 20-year old Herschel Walker, the Heisman Trophy winner out of Georgia, to skip his senior season and sign a multi-year, multi-million contract with New Jersey that stunned the pro football establishment. Walker inked a deal for $16.5 million in February, 1983, which immediately angered the college football world and served notice to the NFL that the USFL was dead serious about being a major league. The signing led to what is now a common practice of college juniors declaring for the NFL Draft, but was scandalous at the time. "My hope is that the NFL will retain its present ruling with regard to underclassmen," Dallas Cowboys head coach Tom Landry told United Press International after Walker made his decision. "I also realize we're in a competitive business and if it comes to a time when our competitors are gaining too great an advantage, then the NFL may have to make a decision to sign underclassmen."

By the time it debuted in March, 1983, the USFL had secured a legendary coach (and, as previously mentioned, one of my favorites) in George Allen (Chicago) as well as other big names such as Chuck Fairbanks (New Jersey), Red Miller (Denver), John Ralston (Denver) and Steve Spurrier (Tampa Bay). And while its early player signings – aside from Walker – didn't rock the sports world, the USFL did manage to lure many well-known NFL players such as former Detroit Lions quarterback Greg Landry (Chicago) and former San Francisco 49ers defensive end Cedrick Hardman (Oakland).

Once the league held its territorial college draft, all the teams had nicknames: the Arizona Wranglers, Birmingham Stallions, Boston Breakers, Chicago Blitz, Denver Gold, Los Angeles Express, Michigan Panthers, New Jersey Generals, Oakland Invaders, Philadelphia Stars, Tampa Bay Bandits and Washington Federals. And unlike the WFL, each club (with Boston the notable exception) was in a "big league" stadium.

As for rule innovations, the most significant were the 2-point conversion option (unavailable in the NFL at the time) and the ability of coaches to challenge plays through the use of instant replay. Kickers were allowed to use one-inch tees on field goals and extra points and in the final two minutes of each half the clock was stopped to move the chains on first downs. As a fan of gimmicks, I was hoping maybe they'd steal the seven-point TD and action point from the WFL, but the USFL was billing itself as being an NFL-like circuit so sticking close to the established rules of the game was a smart move. The inaugural season featured 18 regular season games with no exhibitions, although there were controlled scrimmages. I can't say the arrival of the new league and the new team in my city had quite the same impact as that of the World Football League, but I was still pretty darn happy that Birmingham was back in the pro football business.

BIRMINGHAM STALLIONS
(1983/85)

As you might have guessed by now, I'm one of those people who tends to get inappropriately excited over nicknames and logos, so I was quite anxious about the news conference on June 16, 1982, which would reveal the team owner as well as the "brand." Alabama native and former United States ambassador to Switzerland, Marvin Warner, was named the owner, and he had deep pockets. That's always a good sign. But I was much more interested in the nickname and colors than the name of the man who'd run the team. Originally, Warner said he was leaning toward calling the club the Knights, which wasn't bad (although it made me think more of Birmingham, England, than Birmingham, Alabama). "It's easily symbolized," Warner told the Cincinnati Enquirer. "The cheerleaders could be called the 'Ladies In Waiting.' Or we might run a contest to name the team." He then said there might be a name the team contest, and as defending champion of that particular exercise, I relished the chance to put my mark on another professional football team. I thought then and still think the Birmingham Battalion – wearing Army green, silver and black – is a magnificent nick. Sadly, I never had the opportunity to submit it because no name the team contest was forthcoming. And Warner decided not to go with Knights.

When the big reveal finally came, I was ... underwhelmed. The club would be outfitted in red and gold and be known as the "Stallions," which made sense to Warner because he was a horse breeder. Nothing necessarily wrong with the name, it just didn't have the "punch" I was hoping for, nor did it have anything to do with Birmingham. As for the colors, my first thought was "San Francisco 49ers." I didn't hate the combo nor love it. Then again, if the logo was great, that would cure a lot of ills. I envisioned a herd of Stallions, nostrils blaring as they left dust in their wake. What we got was nothing close to that. It was the silhouette of a horse, and the horse looked tired. Maybe it wasn't really tired, just disinterested. This was a horse who wanted to be left alone. When I saw it, I thought of a cookie – a cookie formed from a horse-shaped cookie cutter. To each his or her own, of course, and I'm sure many people thought it was wonderful. I was not among them. Oh, I'd still buy all the tee shirts and pennants because it was Birmingham's team, but there was nothing exciting about the name or the look. Then came Sept. 2, the day the Stallions named their first head coach.

I had hoped maybe Gotta, back in Canada with the Stampeders, might be convinced to return to Birmingham, but apparently he was never seriously considered and ultimately withdrew his name from consideration. Another name that popped up was that of Dallas Cowboys secondary coach Gene Stallings, who would've been a popular choice based on his Alabama ties and coaching experience. "What bothers me so much is the timing," Stallings told the Associated Press on June 29, 1982. "The Cowboys training camp is about two weeks away and it's hard to walk away. I just wish it was February. Of course, I've made no secret of the fact that I want to be a head coach. But I'm going to need some security and I've got to find out exactly what the owner wants to offer." He was actually offered the job, but turned it down on July 6. "After carefully considering the opportunity, I have asked them to withdraw my name from consideration," Stallings told the Associated Press. "The decision was based on the fact that I am under contract with the Dallas Cowboys and I feel I should honor my commitment." You might remember Stallings did return to the state of Alabama in 1990 to take a high-profile college coaching job.

While a lot of other names were mentioned (including Bobby Bowden and Dan Devine), filling the spot proved to be difficult. Part of the problem might've been Stallions general manager Jim Gould, who – based on news reports at the time – tended to rub people the wrong way. Gotta was one of them, who said he felt "used" by Gould and Stallions officials. "I've been called three times by them and each time they said, 'We'll get back to you tomorrow.' The next day they never called back," Gotta told the Birmingham News. "I've never been treated like that before. There are just certain things that are ethical, even in a goofy business like football. Even burglars have a code of ethics."

I remember Gould's response was that he had "never heard of Gotta" before coming to Birmingham and that the former Ams boss had "hurt himself a little bit" in the WFL. Not sure how winning a championship hurts a coach, and I thought if Gould had never heard of Gotta, perhaps he was working in the wrong town. After just a couple of months Gould resigned to take a job with the Federals, and Jerry Sklar was named the new GM.

And after all the misfires in early September the suspense finally ended when Rollie Dotsch was introduced as the head coach. Rollie Dotsch did not dazzle me. I had no clue what a Rollie Dotsch even was. He was, in fact, an offensive line coach with the Pittsburgh Steelers, and his only head coaching experience came during a stint at Northern Michigan. "Hopefully, we'll build a dynasty here similar to the one we had at Pittsburgh," Dotsch said during his introductory news conference. "Leaving the NFL isn't an easy thing, but I'm delighted to be here. If there's anything I want my football team to be, it's aggressive. I'm a solid coach fundamentally, but I don't mind taking calculated risks. Sometimes I'm on the verge of being reckless. I'll do some things totally unexpected." Certainly, one can look at the NFL and find many assistants who went on to become big names and great successes in the top job. But again, I was hoping for someone who I was familiar with, and Coach Dotsch did not fit that bill. Not to mention the fact that I absolutely hated the Steelers; no real reason why, I just did.

My only hope in the lead up to the 1983 season was that Birmingham would sign some name players. The first signing was Tom Banks, a former Auburn standout as well as All-Pro center with the St. Louis Cardinals, and by Dec. 6 14 former Alabama and Auburn players were under contract, including safety Jim Bob Harris and tight end Bart Krout out of Alabama. To me, though, the biggest "get" in the Stallions' infancy was quarterback Reggie Collier, an All-American out of Southern Miss who had an outstanding college acre that included upsets over Alabama, Ole Miss and Mississippi State.

In 1981 Collier became the first quarterback in NCAA history to run and pass for more than 1,000 yards in a season, rushing for 1,005 yards and 12 touchdowns and throwing for 1,004 yards and six more scores. He was drafted on Jan. 4, 1983 (the third overall pick), and on Jan. 13 he officially became a member of Birmingham's USFL team – signing a contract reportedly worth $2.5 million over five years. "I feel Birmingham is a football town," Collier told the Associated Press. "Also, I want to play quarterback and in the NFL there is some question. I know I can get along with the coaching staff. You can't play if you're not happy." In my mind, that was the Stallions' first "big league" move. This was a player coveted by the NFL who wanted to draft him as a multi-tool athlete, but opting to sign with the new league meant big bucks for him and a shot in the arm to the Magic City's fledgling squad. The contract was signed, sealed and delivered less than two months from the season opener, which was set for March 7 at Legion Field.

The league would debut a day earlier with six Sunday games, while Birmingham's clash with the Michigan Panthers would close out Week One with ESPN's first Monday Night Football telecast of the USFL. Having Birmingham showcased on TV was pretty cool. Seeing the game live and in person, though, would be much cooler.

OPENING NIGHT

After nine years, the band got back together. On WFL opening night in 1974, Pop, Don, Dave and I were at Legion Field for Birmingham's professional football opener. There we were again in 1983, at the same stadium to christen a new Magic City team in a new pro football league. Things had changed quite a bit, of course, especially for me. Instead of a kid seeing my first pro game, I was now a college student working for the school newspaper and – at age 22 – old enough to buy beer and drink it in front of Pop. He was a teetotaler, who once told me that when it comes to beer, "As far as I'm concerned, you can pour it back in the horse." But as long as I wasn't driving and didn't overindulge, he was fine with his youngest son partaking of adult beverages. On this night, though, hot chocolate or coffee was probably the better choice. Unlike the WFL's mid-summer debut, the USFL started in March – and March in Alabama can be quite unpredictable. Instead of shorts and tee shirts, this game required jackets and ponchos. Temperatures, I believe, were in the 50s and there was light rain that came and went.

Since it was the grand opening I figured it would still be a packed house, but instead 38,352 folks showed up to see history. That's not a bad crowd (almost 6,000 more that showed up to see Birmingham win the World Bowl in 1974), but it was the lowest among all the USFL debut games that weekend. For a city that made the Americans and Vulcans WFL attendance leaders, it was puzzling. But truth be told, if I had known the game would play out as it did, I don't think I would've gone, either. Michigan won it, 9-7, and it ranks as one of the most boring sporting events I've ever sat through.

"Offensively, I don't think we were just quite sure where we wanted to go with the football," Dotsch told the Anniston Star afterward. "One game doesn't mean anything. We've got 17 games to go. I feel better about my football team than I did a week ago." Maybe I was distracted; the day before I had covered the Sun Belt Conference Basketball Tournament where UAB defeated South Florida to secure an automatic bid to the NCAA Tournament. That meant I'd get to travel with the team to scenic Evansville, Indiana, for the first round of the Mideast Regional. As March Madness took the sports spotlight, I was in a basketball state of mind. Still, I was excited about my hometown's new football team, until this particular clash gave me reason not to be. All of the Panthers' points came off the leg of kicker Novo Bojovic, who connected from 49, 49 and 48-yards, all in the first half. The Stallions' only score came when Collier scooted in for a short TD in the second quarter, briefly giving Birmingham the lead. Collier injured his hip during the game, which put a big dent in Birmingham's offensive plans.

By the time the third quarter started, we were all cold and wet and the only real entertainment was Pop, who in his yellow rain jacket from a decade earlier still looked like Foghorn Leghorn's nephew. That wasn't enough to keep us in the stands, though. We opted to head to the car and listen to the game on the radio while driving home, and then catch the last quarter on TV. Turns out we didn't miss anything scoring-wise. I was disappointed more in the experience than I was the outcome. While both teams had some good young players and former NFL guys who still had some skills, I expected more than what I got. I guess there was part of me who was hoping to conjure the same thrill I got when I saw the Americans take the field for the first time nine years earlier. But hey – this was the first week of a new league, so maybe things would get better.

AN UP AND DOWN SEASON

My hopes of seeing Collier become the league's QB stud ended quickly when he was injured in the opener, started splitting time with backup Bob Lane, and saw his season end with a Week 10 knee injury. Fortunately, Lane – who started just one game at LSU and then transferred to Louisiana-Monroe (then Northeast Louisiana) where he was a backup QB – was becoming a crowd favorite thanks to his gritty play. Although there was nothing spectacular about his skills, he still managed to help breathe life in the Stallions offense. Even so, there was never a point in the season when Birmingham appeared to be an elite team. Its first win came the second week of the season with a 20-14 overtime victory at Oakland, but in week three the Stallions remained winless at home, falling 17-10 to Philadelphia – this time in front of just 12,850 fans. They followed that up by halting their Legion Field skid with a 16-7 conquest of Arizona, but only 5,000 people bothered to come to the game, which was played in a downpour. (I remember thinking the Americans-Fire game in 1974 was played in an even bigger downpour, and drew almost 55,000 fans). Attendance-wise, Birmingham was looking less and less like a pro football town, despite its reputation as one. After sitting at 2-2 the Stallions lost three straight (27-16 at Boston, 22-11 at Chicago and 9-7 against Denver at home). Birmingham added a bit of star power when it signed former Steelers wideout Jim Smith six games into the season, and he was certainly needed: after seven games Birmingham had a 2-5 record and the buzz around the team was nonexistent – at least as far as I could tell.

New teams can win your heart merely by existing, but to keep it they need to win. And Birmingham's third "major" pro football team was starting to lose me. But then the Stallions started a five-game winning streak with a 21-19 victory over Oakland on April 24. A 35-3 win over Washington, 22-7 victory over New Jersey, 35-20 decision over Los Angeles and 23-20 revenge win at Michigan improved the record to 7-5, and put Birmingham back in the playoff hunt. They had my attention again. "Our players believe now," Dotsch told Associated Press after the win over the Panthers. "They believe in themselves and what we're trying to do. We may or may not get to the playoffs this year, but we're laying down an awfully good foundation."

The Stallions, in fact, didn't qualify for the postseason. The lost their next two (21-19 at Denver and 45-17 at Tampa Bay), beat Boston at home (31-19), and fell to Chicago (29-14) and Philadelphia (31-10) before closing the season with a 29-17 victory over the Bandits in front of 20,300 fans at Legion Field. Sadly, I was apparently a jinx for the club, because it lost the two other games I saw it play live (Denver and Chicago).

Yet while Birmingham underwhelmed in its first season in terms of wins and losses (9-9), there were bright spots. Scott Norwood (for any Buffalo Bills fans who picked this book up by mistake, he is, indeed, THAT Scott Norwood), was one of them, making 25 field goals as well as 34 of 35 extra points. Perhaps the best news came when it was announced during halftime of the season finale that former Auburn running back and Buffalo Bills All-Pro Joe Cribbs would join the team in 1984. I liked the direction the USFL was heading as an organization; while the WFL was a Dead League Walking after its first season, it appeared that USFL owners had the money and the will to ride this thing out and make it work. Attendance wasn't mind-blowing, but it was decent. Denver averaged more than 40,000 fans per game and Tampa Bay, New Jersey and Oakland seated more than 30,000 fans on average for each home contest. Both attendance and TV ratings slipped over the final weeks of the season (average league attendance for the year was 25,214), and it was reported that owners lost roughly $30 million, with only Denver, Oakland and Tampa Bay finishing in the black. But no one expected to get rich in the first season, and those financial figures were not a deterrent for owners who wanted in. The cost of a franchise had increased from $1.5 million to $6 million in a year, but obviously those who coveted teams thought it was a good investment. It didn't hurt that – according to report in the Los Angeles Times in July, 1983 – ABC grossed $82 million after paying USFL rights money. If the spring league took root, then the TV money would start to trickle down.

Surprisingly, the USFL decided to add six more franchises in 1984: the Houston Gamblers, Jacksonville Bulls, Memphis Showboats, Oklahoma Outlaws, Pittsburgh Maulers, and San Antonio Gunslingers. In addition, the Breakers moved from Boston to New Orleans. Trading in tiny Nickerson Field for the palatial Superdome. The weirdest move of the offseason came when the Chicago Blitz and Arizona Wranglers actually "swapped" franchises – players, coaching staffs and all.

Having been burned before, I wasn't about to suggest the USFL or the Birmingham Stallions (averaging 22,000 fans per game) were here to stay. But while the WFL had franchises fold and move during its first season, this league was already expanding by 50 percent heading into year two. Thus, spring football hinted that it might have some staying power, and that was reason for optimism.

CLIFF WHO?

Although I had high hopes that he would be the face of the franchise, it became clear that wasn't in the cards for Collier, who spent his first season as a pro battling injuries. So, it came as no surprise when the Stallions dealt him to the Federals before the start of the 1984 season. Lane had earned the starting job anyway and, from a public relations standpoint, had also earned the support of fans. But Dotsch apparently wasn't fully satisfied with Lane, so he called on his Pittsburgh connections once more – this time for a new quarterback. Cliff Stoudt had taken over for Terry Bradshaw after the Steelers icon was sidelined for the 1983 season, but he didn't exactly endear himself to the faithful there. Although he led the team to 10 wins and a playoff berth, he also ranked 29th among NFL quarterbacks, with 12 touchdowns and 21 interceptions. His biggest sin was not being Bradshaw, of course, and there was no tearful farewell when he decided to jump to the spring league.

As for me, I was actually angered by the signing. Like many other Stallions fans, I had become a big supporter of Lane, and thought with the addition of Cribbs in the backfield, the makings were there for a good offense. But Stoudt wasn't brought in to be a backup, so it was clear that Lane – through no fault of his own – was headed back to the bench. Stoudt, 28, was officially a Stallion in January 12, 1984. "I'm pleased as punch to be here," Stoudt said. "I think this team has a great future. I have a lot of confidence in myself and look forward to the team going all the way to the championship."

My first peek at the new look Stallions came on Feb. 11, 1984, when they played the Breakers and won, 30-10. I remember little about the game other than I had gotten free tickets somehow and there was a very small crowd on hand. Also, being the romantic that I was, I was on a date. I was much more concerned with not having bun chunks fly from my mouth than how Stoudt and Lane stacked up in a glorified scrimmage. Lane was 8-9-0 for 75 yards a touchdown while Stoudt finished 9-13-1 with 74 yards and a TD. My date was also a rousing success, at least in the sense that there was no incident involving food. But the regular season opener at home against the Generals was another story.

BIG CROWD, BAD PERFORMANCE

The largest crowd in Stallions history greeted the team on Feb. 26 when the Generals, led by Walker and former NFL standout QB Brian Sipe, came to Legion Field. It also felt like football season – temperatures were in the low 60s by kickoff and there was enough of a sustained breeze to keep you nice and cold.

Of special interest to me was getting to see first-year New Jersey coach Walt Michaels roam the visitors' sidelines. As a Jets fan, I was quite familiar with his six-year head coaching stint in New York, where he was the architect of the "New York Sack Exchange." Before that he was the defensive coordinator that helped the Jets stun the Baltimore Colts in Super Bowl III, so I was eternally in his debt even if he was on the enemy sideline. The 62,300 fans on hand was both a league and team record, and with the game shown nationally on ABC, Stoudt, Cribbs and their teammates had the chance to show the country Birmingham was ready to get serious about pro football again.

It was a bust – at least for those of us who were cheering for the home team. Pop, Don and I watched Stoudt spend much of the game misfiring (he collected a grand total of 51 yards through the air with an interception, completing just six pass attempts), while Cribbs never could get in a groove, grinding out 52 rushing yards on 16 totes. The hosts' only points came on a pair of Norwood field goals, one in the second quarter and the last in the fourth. Sipe, on the other hand, was quite efficient, while running back Maurice Carthon stole the thunder from Walker with a pair of touchdowns.

Fans booed Stoudt and screamed, "We want Lane!" (I was one of them), and Lane finally got in at quarterback in the second half, giving us a bit of hope and reason to cheer. He finished 13 of 27 for 143 yards, but it was too little, too late. When the contest mercifully ended, Birmingham was on the sad end of a 17-6 score line. "Technically, New Jersey was sounder," Dotsch told the Associated Press. "We couldn't muster enough points. We weren't very sharp ... we certainly didn't play up to our potential offensively. Defensively, we played pretty well."

My streak of having never seen the Stallions win a game that counted was intact, and the desire of my father to follow the USFL was, basically, finished. "I think I'm done," Pop said as we left the stadium. "I don't like crowds, and I don't like watching football in the spring." I couldn't blame him ... if you were staking your fandom on this one game, you probably wouldn't come back. But as unenjoyable as it was, I was becoming impressed with the USFL's star power. Owners were spending money to get established NFL players as well as recent college stars, and I figured that even if the Stallions stunk, I would still get to see some major league football players come to the Football Capital of the South. It was a case of me embracing the league more than the hometown team in the league, but hopefully I could learn to love both equally before the season ended. I could. And I did.

NINE IN A ROW

Birmingham's road to redemption began with a 21-14 victory over Los Angeles in week two, and the Stallions improved to 2-1 when they won 30-18 at Pittsburgh. That game "highlighted" by Stoudt being pelted with snowballs from the fans at Three Rivers Stadium. "The crowd really fired me up," Stoudt told The Sentinel newspaper of Carlisle, Pennsylvania. "I was just excited out there. I was having fun, and I wanted them to know it." The 53,000-plus Mauler supporters should've probably aimed at Cribbs; he rushed for 191 yards and scored a pair of touchdowns to spark the visitors. The next time I saw Birmingham live came on March 17 when the Showboats came to Legion Field. And this time, I actually saw the Stallions win.

Birmingham dominated, 54-6, and Stoudt was clearly the star, throwing for 273 yards and two touchdowns while rushing for two more TDs. This was the first time I got an "AFL vibe" while watching the USFL – seeing a team just let it rip and have a good time doing it. Birmingham scored on every possession of the first half and turned in arguably the best all-around performance in franchise history. "The key to tonight was what happened last week in Pittsburgh," Stoudt told the Anniston Star. "They threw snowballs and beer cans at us, but we pulled together as a team and did what we had to do. We came together this week. This is one of the most perfect examples of team effort in all my years of football."

By the time I left the stadium, I was a fan of Stoudt. His great performance didn't hurt matters, but the good humor he showed after the game against the Maulers and the fact that he never acted as though he was owed the starting job. Regardless, he was quickly becoming one of the top signal callers in the league. As much as I liked Lane, and I finally had to admit that Dotsch knew what he was doing. And maybe I was even starting to think he was a pretty good head coach, too. This was a team and coaching staff that I was proud to call my own.

Wins followed against Tampa Bay (27-9), New Orleans (31-17) and Jacksonville (24-17), and on April 15 Birmingham traveled to greater Detroit and defeated the Panthers, 28-17. Before I watched that game I heard about a story in the New York Times that concerned me a bit. Apparently, Generals owner Donald Trump had been talking to other owners about moving the USFL to a fall schedule in the coming years. I hoped it was just talk; the whole point of the USFL was to play quality football in the spring and give gridiron fans a chance to enjoy the sport 12 months out of the year and not have to worry about testing their loyalties. And wouldn't going head-to-head with the NFL be suicide? Bassett immediately trashed the idea, and maybe his opinion would carry weight if discussion of a season switch ever got serious. "I'm livid about it," Bassett told the Associated Press in an April 16, 1984 story. "I'm trying to renegotiate a television contract and to have this come out at this time is like shooting me in the stomach with a machine gun. To release a falsehood that the league has voted to do this is totally irresponsible." By the time Birmingham hosted Oklahoma a week later – my next chance to visit the Gray Lady – I was thinking about nothing but watching some really good football. Once again, the Stallions delivered, routing Doug Williams and the Outlaws, 41-17. By this time Birmingham had established itself as one of the better teams in a pretty good league, and the coaching of Dotsch and quarterbacking of Stoudt were major reasons for the success.

The winning streak reached nine before Birmingham lost big to Philadelphia, 43-9, and the Stallions closed out the regular season with wins over Jacksonville (42-10), Chicago (41-7) New Orleans (31-14), Washington (42-21) and Memphis (35-20), and loses coming against Arizona (38-28) and Tampa Bay (17-16).

The Stallions were Southern Division champions of the Eastern Conference – and playoff bound with a 14-4 worksheet. There was some drama during the regular season; Cribbs and the Stallions were involved in a contract dispute that resulted in the Stallions suing the running back and Cribbs briefly walking away from the team in May. However, the sides eventually worked through their issues, Cribbs returned, and he ended the season as the USFL's leading rusher with 1,467 yards.

PLAYOFF TIME

Although I had followed various iterations of Birmingham pro football since 1974, I had never been to a postseason game. That changed on July 1, 1984, when Steve Spurrier brought his Tampa Bay Bandits to Legion Field for an Eastern Conference semifinal game. The teams split their regular season games. In fact, Tampa Bay had come to Legion Field just a week earlier and topped Birmingham, 17-16. But the postseason gave both teams a clean slate, and I slathered myself in 30 SPF sunscreen so I could watch what I hoped would be a great day for the Stallions. Indeed, it was. Danny Miller had replaced Norwood as the kicker, and made six field goals on the hot afternoon. Stoudt scored two rushing touchdowns and Cribbs added a third, and the Stallions never trailed in a 36-17 romp. "I knew they were ready today," Dotsch told the Montgomery Advertiser. "I could just feel it in my bones. We had a very tough week of practice, and I guess they were just anxious to play. They were ready, though ... no doubt about it."

Spurrier had made the Bandits one of the league's most exciting teams with his early version of the Fun n' Gun offense, but the Birmingham defense had evolved into one of the USFL's best units. It was a fun, if scorching, afternoon for me and 32,000 of my closest friends, but the downside of the conquest meant the Stallions would next face the Stars. Philadelphia had the best regular season record in the league in 1983, going

15-3, but stumbled against the Panthers in the USFL Championship Game. The 1984 version was even better, going 16-2 (including a 32-point shellacking of the Stallions at Legion Field). While I could've hung back at my low-rent efficiency apartment and done the "lonely fan" thing, I visited Pop on July 8 so he and I could watch the game together. The caveat being that he would listen to a crackly, AM broadcast of the Atlanta Braves vs. Philadelphia Phillies baseball game on his transistor radio at the same time. No matter; I had low hopes of a Stallions upset at Franklin Field, and the game was never close. While the 20-10 final looks respectable, I spent much of the telecast cursing the television. Birmingham turned the ball over four times – with Stoudt tossing three interceptions – and by halftime Philly had built an insurmountable 20-0 lead. All of the Stallions' points came in the fourth quarter, and when it was over the visitors had managed just 220 yards of total offense, with Stoudt suffering six sacks. "We fell behind and then fought back," Dotsch told the Anniston Star. "Our offense didn't play well – their defense knocked us crazy. We just came up a little bit short. We had some guys play their hearts out and other guys not quite play up to their capabilities. It's a disappointing way to end a great season, and it has been a great season."

Obviously, I wasn't happy with the result, but it was one I fully expected. When I looked at the Stars, I saw a team that I think could've been a .500 club in the NFL. They would only get better, and I was confident Birmingham would get better, too.

Almost as soon as the game ended I was already looking forward to the 1985 season, and it would take a lot to curb my enthusiasm. I had no clue the third year of the USFL would be its last.

SIGNS OF TROUBLE

As I got more immersed in the on-the-field activities of the Stallions, I wasn't paying nearly as much attention to what was going on behind the scenes. I thought all that talk of moving to a fall slate would blow over, and I also assumed all the teams in the league were stable. That view was far too optimistic. Just five weeks after the Stars won the USFL title with a 23-3 victory over Arizona, the majority of league owners voted to move to a fall schedule beginning with the 1986 season. Bassett opposed the decision, and joined Denver owner Doug Spedding in voting against it. "The NFL really hoped we'd stay in the spring," USFL Commissioner Chet Simmons told reporters following the announcement. "But moving to fall shows a belief in this product and a belief in this league. The USFL is ready, willing and able to compete for the attention of fans (in the stadium) and television viewers." Trump, who proudly said he was "the instigator" of the talks to remake the league, helped convince virtually every owner that the move would be lucrative. Fall was football season, he said, and that's where the money was, he promised.

Bassett, who was battling cancer, eventually sold his interest as managing partner of the Tampa Bay franchise and vowed to start another spring league. "I'm not going to sit back and let people who don't know how to run their business tell me what to do," Bassett, who claimed to have up to 11 teams lined up for a spring league, told the Associated Press on April 29, 1985. "I think the chances of the USFL succeeding are very slim." I agreed with him completely, and as a fan of both Bassett and spring football I was hoping Birmingham would be part of the league he was creating. Alas, it never materialized. All the drama and uncertainty contributed to the 1985 USFL looking quite different from the league I had grown to love. By the time it began play in 1985, it was down to 14 teams. The Express, which barely drew flies at the L.A. Coliseum, was turned over to the league when its owner went bankrupt. Even though the franchise stayed in Los Angeles, it was anything but healthy.

The Maulers lost more than $10 million and merged with the Stars, which moved to Baltimore. The Oakland and Michigan franchises combined, with the team competing as the Oakland Invaders. The Outlaws merged with the Wranglers and the franchise was rebranded as the Arizona Outlaws. The Breakers moved for the third time in three years, this time to Portland, and the Federals headed to Orlando and were rechristened the Renegades. The Chicago Blitz folded outright, although league officials said the Windy City would receive a future expansion franchise (the original TV contract with ABC stipulated that the league had to have teams in the New York, Chicago and Los Angeles television markets).

The contraction and relocation made sense when framed by the move to a fall schedule. I mean really ... were Eagles, Lions, Steelers, Bears and Saints fans suddenly going to switch their allegiances to the Stars, Panthers, Maulers, Blitz and Breakers?

Not a chance. "It's the worst thing they could've done," quarterback Jim Kelly – still with the Gamblers – told the Associated Press. "But it's up to the major owners. They pay us, so we'll play when they say." And that's what upset the rabid football fan in me the most. With the USFL, you didn't have to choose between leagues. You could enjoy the NFL, too, and see good football winter, spring, summer and fall. Trying to go head to head with the big boys was sports suicide, and anyone who thought differently was in denial. The NFL was the undisputed king of professional football, and had cornered the market on every major market in the United States after merging with the American Football League in 1970. Add the popularity (and ubiquity) of college football on TV, and I didn't see any way the league could find a foothold in the traditional season. The reason the USFL was carving out a niche – and the reason it was given lucrative television contracts right from the start – was that it had football all to itself during baseball season and gave networks fresh programming in a time of year when it was lacking. But then the more I heard people like Trump talk, the more I came to believe there was no earnest intention of creating a true rival league at all.

The fact that the USFL decided to go head-to-head with the senior circuit meant its owners had taken on a "if you can't beat 'em, join 'em" stance. They just wanted a merger, and with all the young stars in the league (players like Steve Young, Kelly, and – coming in 1985 – Doug Flutie), they felt they were in a good position to make that happen. In the case of Trump – long before he became better known for reality TV and the presidency – it was pretty clear to me his goal was getting the Generals in the NFL. I doubt he had much concern for the other teams in the USFL. So less than two months after the owners meeting that changed the course of the soon-to-be-former spring league, Trump and company filed an antitrust suit against the NFL, aimed to break up its monopoly on professional football and seeking damages of $567 million. Under antitrust law that number would be tripled to $1.7 billion, so USFL officials were counting on a jury to give it a major financial victory against the NFL that would provide enough capital to secure passage to the fall – and gain access to a major TV network. But in the words of "The Wire" character Omar Little, "You come at the king, you best not miss."

ONE MORE SPRING FLING

It can be hard to follow a lame duck team, and I couldn't help but think the Stallions were exactly that in

1985. If the USFL won its lawsuit against the NFL and broke up the monopoly, it might force the NFL's hand in a merger. But that didn't mean Birmingham would be part of it. As a fan I had been down this road before when the National Hockey League absorbed four WHA franchises in 1979 – a mini-merger that left out my beloved Birmingham Bulls. Instead of seeing Birmingham play the Montreal Canadiens and New York Rangers at the Birmingham-Jefferson Civic Center, I had to settle for clashes against the Tulsa Ice Oilers and Salt Lake City Golden Eagles as the Bulls dropped down to the Central Hockey League. The NFL already had 30 franchises and my theory (grounded in realism with a healthy dose of pessimism) was that if it acquired six USFL clubs and expanded to 36 teams, the Stallions would not be one of them. Going by on the field performance Birmingham would've been a great addition, but the Magic City was not a major television market. And in professional sports, TV is everything. With franchises in Atlanta and New Orleans, I just couldn't see the NFL wedging one between those Deep South metropolises, even if it came fully stocked and ready to play.

If they did dip back into southern waters, I figured Memphis would've gone ahead of Birmingham. And there was no "Central Football League" for the Stallions to fall back on if they were denied entry in the big league. Plus, there was the "Alabama and Auburn" factor: A Birmingham team in the NFL would play on Sundays, but the roots of Crimson Tide and Tiger fandom ran deep. Perhaps their weekend football money would still be spent on college football. And Birmingham wasn't selling out Legion Field; crowds of 30,000 that were fine in the USFL wouldn't cut it in the NFL. Yet, I held out hope that I was wrong. What if the remaining owners of the USFL, like the "Foolish Club" of the AFL, really and truly wanted to bring a second major professional football league to the fall? I didn't believe it, but I decided to spend the spring and summer of 1985 in denial and root for the Stallions as though they would be a part of my life for the rest of it. And when I kept my focus on the playing field, the season was a whole lot of fun.

Birmingham's one preseason game at Legion Field came on February 16 when the Houston Gamblers came in for a Saturday afternoon game. As always, I was unconcerned with the outcome because the outcome didn't matter, but I was interested to see Kelly quarterback Houston. He did not disappoint, throwing for 156 yards and a touchdown while splitting time with Todd Dillon. The Gamblers won, 20-10, but the first game of the season that would count – and that I counted on being at – came on February 24 when the Stallions hosted the Generals. New Jersey not only had Walker on the roster, but this season he would share the spotlight with Flutie, fresh from a Heisman Trophy-winning campaign at Boston College and one of the most exciting players in the game.

I was pumped and primed for this battle, and had bought my ticket well before the season started because I figured this one might just give Legion Field (and the USFL) another record crowd. Guess what? I missed it ... missed it all. Why did I miss it? Because a date that started in Birmingham in the middle of the day on February 23 somehow wound up in Memphis in the middle of the night. I won't bore you with an abundance of specific details, but let's just say I experienced real blues on Beale Street, was introduced to peppermint schnapps, and found myself eating bacon and eggs around 11 a.m., February 24, in Tupelo, Mississippi, at a restaurant I cannot name because its name is one I cannot remember. I can name the server though; she was Gertie, and she was magnificent. At the time the unplanned road trip was worth it. I had a blast. And while football was still a very important part of my life, I had learned that – at age 24 – there was much, much more to life.

But dang, I missed a good one – well, at least it was a good one if you were Stallions fan.

As I learned when I read about the game in Monday's Birmingham News, Flutie struggled, the Generals' vaunted rushing attack was held to 111 yards, and Stoudt was outstanding in engineering a 38-28 victory of the home team.

Birmingham led 31-7 in the third quarter and were never threatened by the star-laden club from Jersey. "All we heard and read all week was Flutie and the New Jersey Generals," Stoudt said. "Even our own media was doing it. The city boys with their Heisman Trophies were going to come to Alabama and show these country boys from Alabama. Right now, down deep inside, I'm grinning." Stoudt certainly beat Flutie on the stat sheet, but the stat that stood out the most, however, was attendance. The crowd was 34,785, which was pretty good by league standards but disappointing when you considered the Stallions drew more than 60,000 fans when they opened against the Generals a year earlier. I really thought the "Flutie factor" was enough to make Legion Field mostly full, but perhaps I wasn't the only person getting the lame duck vibe from the team (and league). Whatever the case, going forward I vowed to steer clear of Memphis on days preceding Stallions home games. And, just to be safe, I also vowed to steer clear of peppermint schnapps forever.

PLAYOFF RUN

The Stallions didn't exactly build on the opening day win, losing at home to Denver in Week Two, 40-23. However, Birmingham reeled off four consecutive victories after that. The Stallions beat Orlando, 34-10, Memphis, 34-19, Baltimore, 7-3 and Jacksonville, 25-18. The biggest during that stretch – to me, anyway – was the upset of the Stars in Baltimore. The defending league champions were the USFL gold standard, and the fact that the Stallions were able to go on the road and pull off the victory made me think perhaps my team was developing some championship-caliber credentials. "The big thing was how we beat them," Dotsch told the Baltimore Sun. We shut them down just the way they did to us in the past. "Credit our players with overcoming their concerns with what's going on with ownership. This was a 60 minute tug-of-war, and we beat them in the trenches." There were, indeed, ownership questions, so the club's winning ways were overshadowed by trouble at the bank. Warner's Home State Savings Bank, which he founded in the early 1970s, went bankrupt due to fraud, and he lost millions of dollars. He was forced to transfer his interest in the franchise at the end of March. (In 1987 Warner was sentenced to three and half years in prison and fined $22 million for his part in the scandal. He ultimately served two and a half years.)

Warner's exodus put the Stallions on shaky ground early in the season, and prompted the Birmingham City Council to "invest" $1 million in the franchise to keep it afloat. There was also a rumor that North Carolina businessman George Shinn wanted to buy the franchise and move it to Charlotte, so the bailout might thwart a relocation scenario. "I think we're all grateful to the mayor and city council for this show of confidence," Dotsch told the Associated Press. "It makes me, the staff and the team feel better about it. It was getting pretty tight and this is a very positive sign. Hopefully, we can work our way out from here."

Obviously, I didn't want the Stallions to fold or leave, so I guess the fan in me breathed a sigh of relief when the city came to their rescue. But the taxpayer in me wasn't happy about it all. While I was already worried about the future of the USFL as a whole, this made me wonder if Birmingham would even be a part of it should the league survive the move to a fall slate.

But the cash infusion – whether I approved of it or not – meant the players got paid and the games went on as scheduled, at least for 1985. And if the USFL won its lawsuit, there'd be plenty of money to go around anyway. So yet again I tried to push the negative stuff toward the back of my mind, and simply enjoy good football. After the four-game run Birmingham struggled a bit, losing to San Antonio, 15-14, beating Oakland, 20-17, and Tampa Bay, 30-3, before falling to Jacksonville, 27-17, and Memphis, 38-24. The loss to the Showboats put the Stallions at 7-4, but in the season's final regular season stretch, the team hit its stride. I made a point to spend a lot of time at Legion Field during Birmingham's playoff run, and was determined to be in the stands once the postseason began.

The Stallions closed out the regular season with six wins in seven games, downing Portland, 14-0, Los Angeles, 44-7, Orlando, 41-17, Houston, 29-27, Baltimore, 14-7 and New Jersey, 14-6, with their only loss a 17-14 setback to Tampa Bay in the penultimate game. The second win over the Stars, completing a regular season sweep of the defending USFL champions, had me thinking Birmingham might just be good enough to win its second pro football title. "I haven't been here too long," Dotsch told the Montgomery Advertiser after his team's 14-7 victory over Baltimore at Legion Field, "but if there's been better defense played at Legion Field, I'd like to see it. It was a gross injustice not to get the shutout." They won the Eastern Conference title with a 13-5 record, and that meant as long as they kept winning, they'd host every playoff game up until the 1985 USFL Championship Game at the Meadowlands in New Jersey. Up first were the Gamblers, who were the last qualifier out of the Western Conference with a 10-8 record.

I had seen Kelly and company way back in February for their exhibition victory at Legion Field, but on June 29 I expected a better outcome. I got it, with Miller kicking five field goals – the last coming with two minutes to play – to lift Birmingham to a 22-20 victory and a spot in the Eastern Conference Championship Game against Baltimore. "I felt good when I hit it," Miller told the Montgomery Advertiser. "I didn't watch it. I don't think I picked up my head until it was in the net." Houston kicker Tony Fritsch had a chance to win it for the visitors on the final play, but his 49-yard effort was wide left. "We got the kicks when it counted and they didn't," Dotsch said. "It's something when the whole season comes down to one play like that. If the people out there didn't like that game, I don't know what they'll like." I'd love to tell you that it was a rollicking crowd that packed the stadium and led the home team to victory, but that was not the case. At all. Only 18,500 people bothered to show up for what was, at the time, the biggest game of the year.

To be fair, though, most of the news surrounding the USFL was bad. ABC was withholding money from the league because it was moving teams out of markets that had been agreed upon during contract negotiations. And if the USFL was going forward with a fall schedule, ABC would not be part of it – taking its $50 million TV contract with it. The Stallions continued to have financial problems as well, and there was much uncertainty over who would take control of the franchise with Warner out of the picture. In reality, there were serious money issues throughout the league. Had I been playing closer attention to the stories involving USFL finances, I'd have realized that maybe it wasn't all that stable even before the decision to abandon the spring. It's easy to say now, of course, because we're all psychics when it comes to predicting the past. But when Baltimore came to Legion Field on July 7 to play Birmingham for the Eastern Conference crown, I had a gut feeling it would be the last time I ever saw the Stallions live.

LAST HURRAH

By the time the postseason commenced, I thought Oakland and Birmingham were the best two teams in the league, and on track to play each other for the championship. Once the playoff quarterfinals were over, the Invaders had the best record in the USFL at 14-4-1, while Birmingham sat at 14-5. When Baltimore came to town they were sporting an 11-7-1 record, which was subpar for a team that played for the first USFL title and one the second championship game in league history. They still had a great coach in Jim Mora and a game-breaking running back in Kelvin Bryant, but I was confident they'd find themselves overmatched against the Stallions. In fact, Birmingham swept Baltimore during their two regular season games. So, my niece's husband and me donned our best summer attire (sadly, that would be jorts and tee shirts) and trekked to Legion Field, where we bought tickets on site and wound up sitting near the 50-yard line because only 23,250 fans were inside the 76,000-seat venue. That didn't exactly create a home field advantage for the Stallions, and I remember the crowd seemed disengaged. Then again, there was nothing to keep them engaged because the Stars put this one away early.

Baltimore scored first when Jonathan Sutton turned a first quarter Stoudt interception into a pick six. Later in the frame, Stars QB Chuck Fusina connected with Victory Harrison on a 30-yard touchdown play, and the visitors were up 14-0 in the first quarter. Things got worse before halftime. Fusina found Bryant out of the backfield on a 70-yard scoring play, and at 21-0 this one was over for all practical purposes. Bryant added Baltimore's fourth score with a 76-yard power jaunt that made it 28-0 in the fourth quarter, and that dagger convinced a lot of fans to escape the scorching heat and take it to the house. I decided to stay until the final horn. I had no illusions that the Stallions would mount a stunning 11th hour comeback – they were whipped – but this was the last spring football game I'd ever see them play and, quite possibly, the last time they'd play at all. The final score was a respectable 28-14, with Joey Jones catching a 14-yard TD toss from Stoudt and Cribbs adding a 1-yard touchdown (and Miller toeing the PAT) to wrap up Stallions offensive output for 1985. "You've got to give credit to Baltimore," Dotsch said in the postgame press conference. "They performed very well in the game today and we didn't perform as well. We got behind early and that's a tough situation to recover from against a team like Baltimore. They showed why they're champions and we aren't there yet. But I'm extremely proud of our staff and players. There's no quit in this team."

This one hurt on a couple of levels. From a strictly football standpoint, I thought the Stallions were the better team and should've give a better performance in their most important contest of the year. But there was also a sense of sadness because this didn't just feel like the end of a season, but the end of an era. The entire existence of the USFL now hinged on a lawsuit, and if a merger came I was doubtful Birmingham would be in the mix. "I don't know about the future of the league, the players, the coaches or the team, but I'm extremely proud of our staff and players for the way we fought back," Dotsch told the Anniston Star after the game. While nothing could ever match the excitement I felt as a 13 year old when the Americans debuted, at age 24 I had come to view the Stallions as a great organization. Stoudt, who I dismissed when he was first signed, had become one of my very favorite players.

Dotsch, who I had panned as a no-name choice when he was hired, earned my respect as one of the best head coaches in the business. Birmingham's WFL club was my team then, but Birmingham's USFL squad was my team now. And I didn't want them to go.

THE WAITING GAME

After the Stars defeated the Invaders to win the league title, there was plenty of USFL news in the coming months – just none that involved actual games. First it was announced that the Gamblers and Generals would merge and play in New York. That meant Kelly would be the "franchise" QB, giving Trump another star-studded addition to a team that had marquee performers but no real marquee success. Franchises for 1986 would be placed in Baltimore, Birmingham, Jacksonville, Memphis, New York/New Jersey, Orlando, Phoenix, Portland and Tampa, with the possibility of an additional city to give the USFL 10 teams. Had that scenario played out, the league would've gone from 12 teams to 18 to 14 to 10 in its four seasons. By December lawyers from both the USFL and NFL met to discuss settling the lawsuit, but NFL owners quickly decided they weren't interested in any kind of merger and were willing to let the lawsuit play out in the courts. On December 11 a resolution was passed that read, "Resolved, that the NFL member clubs have no interest in merger with the USFL or settlement of the USFL lawsuit against the NFL. They directed league attorneys to prepare for trial on the earliest realistic date." Then, in February, 1986 – just seven months before the scheduled

start of the USFL's first fall season – the league
announced it would play with eight teams; Portland
would not be part of the USFL when it re-started. The
schedule was released on May 12, with 72 regular season
games scheduled beginning with Arizona at Tampa Bay
on Saturday, September 13. The September 14 slate
would include Birmingham at Jacksonville and Orlando
at Baltimore, and the game that night featuring New
Jersey at Memphis would be the first ESPN game;
ABC was now out of the picture and the cable network
was the league's only TV partner. The championship
game was set for Sunday, February 1, in Jacksonville.

Looking at the Stallions schedule a couple of things
stood out. Birmingham had three games on Saturdays in
which Alabama and Auburn also played, which would've
certainly impacted attendance. Not for me – I was all-in
with the Stallions – but the reality is a USFL team was
not going to attract the same number of fans as the
Crimson Tide and Tigers. Birmingham was also slated
to host Jacksonville on Christmas Day at 7 p.m. I'm
guessing had I gone to that game (and I would have if I
could) I would've part of an extremely small crowd. But
just because games were scheduled didn't mean games
would be played, and on July 29, the jury rendered its
verdict in the antitrust lawsuit.

HOLLOW VICTORY

I'm not going to waste your time with a lengthy
USFL postmortem. There are already two great books

about it – Jim Byrne's "The $1 League: The Rise And Fall Of The USFL" and "Football For A Buck: The Crazy Rise And Crazier Demise Of The USFL," by Jeff Pearlman. And the 30 for 30 ESPN documentary "Small Potatoes: Who Killed The USFL," is a must-see for anyone who loved the league. The bottom line is that the USFL won its lawsuit, was awarded a dollar, had that award tripled to three dollars, and never played another game. "I can't fathom it," USFL attorney Harvey Myerson told Knight News Service after the verdict. "It's inconceivable. I just don't understand this. I understand reducing damages, but to find them guilty and then give us just one dollar is ridiculous."

Trump – never one to admit defeat even when the game is obviously lost – acted as though the verdict was a triumph. "We won a great moral victory," he said. "But now, with the jury's confusion and what seems to be a hung jury, we expect to win a total victory." Six days after the verdict USFL owners voted to suspend play for the 1986 season, all the players were released from their contracts, and the league folded without officially folding.

"It took us three years to build this franchise and three minutes to lose it," Outlaws co-owner Bill Tatham Jr. told the Associated Press. Oh, there was idle talk about regrouping and reforming for 1987, but you'd have to be a special brand of idiot to think there was any path forward after abandoning the spring and putting all its hopes on a jury. "It's like their decision was to make no decision and to just put everything on hold when we've been on hold for over a year and a half," Flutie told the Associated Press. "It upsets me a little bit that my future is still uncertain and that I'm still on permanent vacation." The official end of the USFL came on March 10, 1988, when an appeals court denied its request for a new antitrust trial against the NFL.

Part of the 2nd U.S. Circuit Court of Appeals ruling reads as follows: The USFL's product was not appealing largely for reasons of the USFL's own doing and that the networks chose freely not to purchase it. The USFL asks us to grant sweeping injunctive relief that will reward its impatience and self-destructive conduct with a fall network contract. It thus seeks through court decree the success it failed to achieve among football fans. In particular, there was evidence that the USFL abandoned its original strategy of patiently building up fan loyalty and public recognition by playing in the spring. Faced with rising costs and some team owners impatient for immediate parity with the NFL, the idea of spring play itself was abandoned even though network cable contracts were available. Some of the new owners, notably Donald Trump, believed the USFL ought to play in the fall. Therefore, the issue of when to play became divisive and several owners came to believe Trump was trying to bring about a merger that would include only some USFL teams. The NFL introduced extensive evidence designed to prove Trump's USFL merger strategy and that strategy ultimately caused the USFL's downfall.

Harry Usher, who served as the USFL's last commissioner, summed up the decision quite succinctly: "I guess we died today," he said. The United States Football League – just like the World Football League before it – was out of business. And for the second time in a decade, a professional football league had broken my heart. "I don't know if we have any grounds to go to the Supreme Court," Usher said. "I'm disappointed, but nothing in this case has surprised me. It's been a convoluted situation. The bottom line is (the courts) denied us relief. I'm sorry for the players and the public and television fans." In January, 1989, at least USFL lawyers were able to cash in when a federal court ruled the NFL had to pay $5.5 million in attorneys' fees stemming from the 1986 lawsuit. They did win the case, after all. "This partially takes the sting out of the jury's (earlier) confused verdict," Usher told the Associated Press. "It's a great feeling to be vindicated." The USFL was also awarded $62,220 in costs. "The judge has once and for all clearly stated that the USFL won the case and has awarded significant fees," Trump told AP. "Our position has not only been vindicated by the judge but by the American public, which has seen all the great USFL players excel in the NFL."

WHAT MIGHT HAVE BEEN

I've spent years singing the praises of the USFL, and will always fantasize that it had the potential to be a legitimate second major football league in America.

Having potential and reaching that potential, however, are two different things. The more I think about it, the less I believe that NFL-caliber competition would've been feasible in a spring/summer circuit. The USFL generated national headlines and made a huge impact by spending big money on stars, but by the third year financial irresponsibility was starting to affect the bottom line. And over time it was bound to lose more battles than it won when it got involved in bidding wars with the NFL. The only real way it could've co-existed with the established juggernaut was to form some sort of an alliance, and that would've likely meant becoming a farm league for the big league. I can't envision a scenario where the leagues shared a draft, and really that would be the only way the USFL could retain major league status over the long haul. I'd love to think that had it stuck to its original plan, a 32-team USFL would be thriving today, giving us great football from February to July. And there's no harm in thinking that since we'll never know.

On the other hand, what if the USFL had been awarded millions in its lawsuit? It might've lasted a year or two before the NFL decided to snatch some franchises and put it out of business. There was no way the "major market" teams of the USFL could lure NFL fans to their side, and the secondary markets in the league would've withered away. Plus, just because it would've had access to a major television network wouldn't have meant that network had to buy the product. Even if it did, how many people would watch it?

The 1986 season was to have the Arizona Outlaws, Jacksonville Bulls, Orlando Renegades and Tampa Bay Bandits in the Independence Division, while the Baltimore Stars, Birmingham Stallions, Memphis Showboats and New Jersey Generals would comprise the Liberty Division. Not a lot of major TV markets in that lineup outside of the New York/New Jersey area, which means not a lot of advertising dollars and, ultimately, a huge roadblock to success. Since the St. Louis Cardinals didn't move to Phoenix until 1988, perhaps the Outlaws would've been coveted by the NFL in a limited merger. Maybe the Bulls, too.

Again, we can only speculate. Dixon's original plan was to avoid throwing away millions of dollars on superstars and build teams from the ground up. The USFL could still have good players, but they would be part of a responsible organization that was built to last. The main point of playing in the spring was to avoid having to squeeze into a season already owned by the NFL and college football. Of course, if USFL owners had stuck with a conservative financial game plan, I'd have never gotten to see guys like Cribbs, Smith and Norwood play for my hometown team. It might've still been enjoyable football, but not elite, major league football.

The USFL was never the NFL, but it wasn't far behind. With each passing season, elite teams like the Stars and Stallions were closing the gap. And hundreds of players who started in the USFL ended their career as NFL stars. Kelly, Young, Reggie White (Memphis Showboats) and Gary Zimmerman, (L.A. Express), are members of the Pro Football Hall of Fame.

A few years ago, I was covering a Clemson football game at Memorial Stadium, and saw Cliff Stoudt near the players' locker room after it was over. His son, Cole, was starting quarterback for the Tigers for eight games during the 2014 season. I was trying to make my way over to him just to tell him how much he and the Stallions meant to me, but before I could, the locker room opened and we had to bum-rush our way in for postgame interviews. I really wish I had been able to talk to him, however briefly. Anyway, Cliff, if you happen to read this, thanks. I'm glad I had the privilege of watching you play.

WORLD LEAGUE OF AMERICAN FOOTBALL

Although the old Continental Football League and Atlantic Coast Football League could be considered unofficial farm systems for the NFL and AFL, such a structure never officially existed until 1991. That was the first year of the World League of American Football, and the first time the NFL had ever put its development stamp on – and money behind – another football league. But in its original incarnation, the WLAF was supposed to be much more. Tex Schramm, who built the Dallas Cowboys into "America's Team," was hoping to build American football into the world's game when he named president of the new league. It would have franchises across the globe, and those in the United States would be, for the most part, in non-NFL cities, although the New York metro area would be represented due to its standing as king of the television and advertising markets.

The NFL owners who were funding the league, however, had other ideas.

Schramm made the mistake of hinting that one day the WLAF could stand alone as a major league, and that's when he was told to stand aside and let someone else run the show. The WLAF media guide gives credit to Schramm for getting the league up and running, but says he "relinquished" his role as president in 1990 to make way for Mike Lynn, then the general manager of the Minnesota Vikings. In fact, Schramm was fired, and once Lynn took over the international league proudly proclaimed itself as a developmental circuit. The groundwork was laid in 1989 when TV networks – perhaps missing the spring programming provided by the USFL – approached the NFL owners about starting a new international league. The WLAF was officially formed on July 1, 1989, with all NFL owners voting unanimously to fund it. "It has been my contention for many years that the rest of the world is ready for American football," said Lynn told Game Time, the league's official magazine. "The economics and governmental environment in Europe has changed dramatically in the last decade, and many new opportunities have presented themselves. In my opinion, and in the opinion of many others, the World League is an idea whose time has come."

While the WFL was a financial disaster and the USFL was also losing millions of dollars by the time it folded, the WLAF controlled expenses through the single entity model; all players, coaches and officials were paid by the league, and the head office also handled all transportation costs. In its inaugural season there were 20 teams divided into three divisions.

The European Division featured the Barcelona Dragons, Frankfurt Galaxy and London Monarchs. The North American East Division was made up of the Montreal Machine, New York/New Jersey Knights,

Orlando Thunder and Raleigh-Durham Skyhawks. The Birmingham Fire, Sacramento Surge and San Antonio Riders comprised the North American West Division. As far as rule changes, there were a few different from the NFL. Two-point conversions, still not allowed in the big league, were an option (the offense would scrimmage from the three-yard line). If the receiving team chose to down a kickoff in its end zone, the ball would be spotted at the 10-yard line. If the kick went out of the end zone, the offense would begin at the 20. The overtime procedure was unique in that the first team to score six points in any combination was the winner. If a team didn't reach that number after 15 minutes of O.T., the one with the most points would be declared the winner. If the score was tied after the extra session, the result remained a tie.

The play clock was reduced from 45 to 35 seconds, and intentional defensive pass interference was a spot foul while the unintentional variety was a standard 15-yard penalty.

Teams played a 10-week regular season from late March to late May, and four teams qualified for the playoffs – the three division champions and a wildcard team that had the best non-division winning record. Games would be televised on ABC and the USA Network. Although WFL fans will tell you that World Bowl I was played on Dec. 5, 1974, in Birmingham, the WLAF media guide insisted that World Bowl I would take place on Jun 9, 1991 at Wembley Stadium in London.

BIRMINGHAM FIRE (1991-92)

As a kid, I embraced the Americans and Vulcans. As a college age adult, the Stallions had my full support. By the time the World League of American Football was formed, though, I was grown man with a full-time job. And luckily for me, that full-time job was sports writer. When I was a youngster I dreamed of playing professional football, but as I grew older I finally realized that a lack of height, a lack of girth and a lack of talent meant that was an impossible dream. But I always loved to write, and getting paid to write about sports was just about the coolest thing I could possibly imagine. So instead of just hearing about the formation of the Birmingham Fire, I got to actually write about the team while working as sports editor of The Daily Home newspaper in Talladega, Alabama. High school sports was our main focus, as was the case with most small to mid-size dailies in the south. But being in Alabama also meant we covered the Crimson Tide and Tigers, so Fridays and Saturdays in the fall were quite football-centric for me. In the spring, prep baseball, softball and track and field were prominent in the sports section, and

Talladega's spring NASCAR race was obviously quite a big deal. Having spring football thrown into the mix might add to the workload, but I wasn't about to complain.

I used to save every newspaper after an Americans, Vulcans and Stallions game, just so I could relive the events through the written word. Now that I was in the business I got to do the writing – and could write about football when I couldn't think of anything else. Having my hometown part of an international gridiron circuit was certainly worth some ink and I was honored to have the chance to provide it. That meant the experience would also be quite different, though, because – when I was on the clock – I couldn't be a fan. Sports writers are supposed to be dispassionate when covering an event; fans get mad when you don't fluff the home team and people who work for the home team sometimes get upset when you don't follow their party line. But, reporters report, promoters promote, and rooters root, and there has to be a separation of powers, so to speak.

So, when I wanted to cheer for the Fire on my own time, that was fine. But when I was working, I had to approach any game or interview like Joe Friday – I just wanted the facts. And the fact is, the WLAF seemed like a league with built-in staying power once it was formed, and that meant success by association when it came to Birmingham. It was officially granted a franchise just under a year before the WLAF played its first season, with Schramm holding a press conference on April 18, 1990. Six months later Gavin Maloof, former owner of the Houston Rockets, was named majority owner of the Birmingham team. "I'm ready to hit the ground running," Maloof said. "I'm confident that the partnership we'll form with the citizens of this area will make us one of the most successful sports franchises in the world." On Dec. 6, Maloof's team became known as the Birmingham Fire. I liked the nickname – it didn't necessarily scream "Birmingham!" but along with earth, water and air, it's certainly one of my favorite elements. Plus, the uniform colors of crimson, navy and gold looked good. The team's helmets were blue with crimson flames trimmed in gold, and up to that point were my favorite lids in the history of pro football in Birmingham. The adjustment, of course, was this was a developmental league.

Whether they actually were or were not, the WFL and USFL aspired to major league status, which included big names who had already been successful in the NFL, or college hot shots who were high draft picks but jumped at the money offered from upstart leagues. The way I saw it, I'd view the Fire the same way I viewed the Birmingham Barons (and before them, the Athletics) of the Southern League. It was AA baseball designed to prepare players for the big leagues, and I enjoyed it very much. There were no illusions that the Fire roster would be stocked with "name" players – I only hoped the coach would be able to put a competitive roster together and help these guys move up to the NFL in the next couple of years.

The coach tasked with doing that was Chan Gailey, who was introduced on December 21, 1990. I was familiar with Gailey due to his stint at Troy State University, where he led the Trojans to the Division II National Championship in 1984. He jumped to the NFL to take an assistant coaching job with the Broncos in 1985, so it made sense that the WLAF came calling. As an offensive coordinator and quarterbacks coach with Denver, I had high hopes Gailey would install a high octane attack and field a team that put plenty of points on the board. The WLAF draft was interesting; a month before the season began coaches gathered in Orlando to make selections from a large pool of players who had already been signed by the league. It was a multi-day event, with offensive linemen chosen on the first day, followed by running backs, punters and kickers, quarterbacks, wide receivers and tight ends, defensive linemen, linebackers, and defensive backs.

GIVE PEASE A CHANCE

I knew a lot of the players Birmingham selected would be completely unfamiliar to me. I had hoped, however, that perhaps some of the skill guys might ring a bell. I was especially anxious to find out who Gailey would sign as his quarterback.

Would it be a guy from a major school, maybe even someone who toiled in the SEC? Nope. It was Brent Pease. When I found out Pease was the selection I had no reaction because at no point in my life had I ever heard of the man. Remember, these were the pre-Internet days, so you didn't have Google or Wikipedia to tell you everything you needed to know. And at that time, I knew nothing about Pease and doubted anyone in the state of Alabama knew anything about him, either. But Gailey talked him up like the former Montana star was going to be the Joe Montana of the WLAF.

During his senior season with the Grizzlies in 1987, he passed for 3,056 yards and 30 touchdowns, which was good enough to get drafted by the Minnesota Vikings in the 11th round of the draft. He was released during training camp, and the only NFL action he saw was as a replacement player for the Houston Oilers in 1987. He was completely out of football when Gailey brought him to Birmingham. Yet the next football game I coach will be the first football game I coach, so I figured Gailey knew what he was doing and I was interested to see Birmingham's newest team come out of the tunnel at Legion Field.

OPENING NIGHT

Legion Field was undergoing an expansion that would increase capacity to 84,000, and part of the reconfiguration meant the press box was of the temporary, open-air variety on the evening of March 23, 1991. That suited me just fine. It was a cool, pleasant evening for what was billed as "Opening Night Around The World," and it felt good to be in the stadium and among the fans for the Fire's home opener against the Montreal Machine. While walking around the outskirts of the field during warm-ups I even ran into my brother, who was working a concession stand to raise money for Springville High School athletics. We joked about the fact that the birth of his first son caused us to miss the inaugural regular season game of the Vulcans. Now his kid was playing high school football – which was the reason he was back at Legion Field to christen another new team in another new league.

Halftime entertainment was to be provided by Jerry Lee Lewis, which I thought was pretty cool. Sure, the guy was 56 years old and hadn't charted in 20 years (his 1972 version of Chantilly Lace"), but he was still "The Killer." Even if the game was subpar I would at least get to brag that I had seen a legend up close and personal. I had no idea what kind of crowd to expect, although my best guess would be in the 25,000 range. Apparently, stadium officials had no idea how many folks to prepare for, either. As opening kickoff approached, thousands of football fans continued to click through the turnstiles, causing a delay in the start time. By the time they settled into their seats, 52,942 fans had decided to show their support for the Fire, which was a phenomenal number considering this was a minor league.

I was thoroughly impressed. And with all those people, there was a real buzz – I thought this might be the start of something special.

The Football Capital of the South once again had expanded its footprint, and now the only question was whether or not the new team could reward their supporters. On this night, they could not. In fact, it would've been difficult to have made a worst first impression. I've seen many boring football games during my time on earth, and while I can't say this was the least entertaining of all, it would at least be a major part of the conversation. Montreal won the game, 20-5, despite amassing only 179 yards of total offense. "The home crowd was great out there," Gailey said. "It appears that everybody did their job out there except us. The city, the organization and the fans were all great. Now we have to do our part next week and give the city what it deserves – a winner."

The Machine's initial points came in the first quarter following a botched punt, with Bjorn Nittmo kicking a 22-yard field goal. Then in the second quarter a snap sailed over the head of Birmingham punter Kirk Maggio, putting Montreal in business at the Fire 17. Kevin Sweeney followed with a two-yard touchdown pass to Keith Jennings, and the visitors led 10-0 at the half. Nittmo's 36-yard field goal in the third frame made it 13-0, but Birmingham finally got on the board in the fourth when former Auburn sidewinder Win Lyle nailed a 35-yard field goal. Birmingham cut the deficit to 13-5 with a safety (making it a one possession game thanks to the availability of a two point conversion), but the Machine put it away in the final two minutes with a one-yard TD plunge by Elroy Harris. Pease hit just 17 of 39 passes for 152 yards. "Offensively we weren't consistent and couldn't hold on to the ball," Gailey said. "But the defense scrapped their fannies off. They didn't play well enough to win, but they played pretty dang good."

From a journalism standpoint, the story – at least from the Birmingham angle – was that the Fire was their own worst enemy due to miscues. My story in The Daily Home began this way: So you think WLAF is an acronym for World League of American Football? Think again. If Saturday night's season opener between Birmingham and Montreal is any indication, the letters stand for Woefully Lacking in the Area of Fundamentals, or possibly Wobbly, Listless Aerial Futility.

The Machine doused the Fire, 20-5, in a contest that suggested the World League is worlds away from showcasing top-flight football. As a fan, I was bummed. I had high hopes that maybe this team – and this league – would bring back my youthful enthusiasm for Brand X football in Birmingham. I could only hope that Pease and company would figure out a way to generate some offense – and some excitement – going forward. I always liked to talk to Pop about all things sports, and remember calling him the next day to get his take on the contest. He wasn't impressed, either. "John McKay (former Southern California and Tampa Bay Buccaneers coach) was asked one time about the execution of his team, and he said, 'I'm all for it,'" Pop joked. "That's what I was thinking when I watched that mess. I'm glad baseball starts in a couple of weeks ... I don't think this league is gonna interest me."

.500 REGULAR SEASON

Fire home attendance was wildly inconsistent in 1991, with the high coming on opening night, the low 8,114 on a rainy April evening against San Antonio, and two games that eclipsed the 30,000 mark – and 30,000 is quite respectable for minor league anything. The team was inconsistent in wins and losses as well, finishing 5-5 and sneaking into the playoffs. They improved to 1-1 with a 17-10 victory over Sacramento on March 30, and the rest of their regular season results came in twos – two losses (23-10 to Montreal and 27-0 to London); two wins (31-6 over Orlando and 16-12 over San Antonio); two more losses (11-6 to Barcelona and 10-3 to Frankfurt); and a two-game winning streak (24-14 over New York/New Jersey and 28-7 over Raleigh-Durham) leading into the playoffs. The season ended with a 10-3 loss to Barcelona, where the Fire treated 40,000-plus fans at Legion Field to six turnovers in yet another game in which the offense was AWOL. For my money – and speaking strictly as a fan – the entertainment value was pretty low. Birmingham scored more than 30 points just once all season, and never broke single digits in all five of its losses, including a shutout defeat at the hands of London. The high-scoring offense promised by Gailey was one of the worst in the league, and Pease was last in the WLAF in passing yardage with 922 yards.

On the plus side, he threw just six interceptions all year.

However, he accounted for only five touchdowns through the air. By season's end I was writing less and less about the Fire because our newspaper's readers didn't seem to care, and from a personal standpoint, I'd largely lost interest as well. I could handle minor league football if it was fun, but fun was sorely lacking in Birmingham's first season in the NFL-funded league.

YEAR TWO

In the months leading up to the Fire's second WLAF campaign, I tried to get "re-hyped" and pay attention to what was going on with the team and the league. That didn't change the fact that my first impression was a bad one, and it was hard to shake as Gailey introduced what he hoped to be a new and improved club in 1992. One positive step was at quarterback; Pease had been shipped to New York/New Jersey, where he would back up former Slack (a former CFL Barracudas backup), while Mike Norseth was the new man behind center in Birmingham.

Norseth had been a solid college quarterback at Kansas, but his NFL career never panned out. He played one season with the Cincinnati Bengals in 1988, appearing in just one game and attempting no passes. The Fire was his last chance to prove himself in the pro ranks. Still, surely it would be a step up. While Pease is now in the midst of a nice coaching career (he is currently assistant head coach and wide receivers coach at Montana), he just didn't get the job done during his time in the Magic City. As training camp opened in Orlando in February, 1992, Gailey said upgrading the offense was at the top of his list. "Obviously, it's an area where we have to improve," he said. "You can play good defense and have good kicking and be a winning team, but you can never win championships without being good in all three phrases."

The coach also said having his staff together for a full year would make a big difference. "It's drastically different," Gailey said. "It's like comparing apples and oranges. Our staff has been together a year now and we feel a lot better about each other. I'm not having to teach the coaches the plays the night before we put them in."

As far as "local heroes," former Alabama kicker Philip Doyle, who prepped at Birmingham's Huffman High School, was on the roster, as was former Auburn linebacker Greg Ogletree. But most of the rest of the lineup featured NFL castoffs and players Birmingham football fans didn't know, and that lack of familiarity proved to be box office poison. The Fire's largest crowd was 20,794 when the Sacramento Surge came to town, a game that Birmingham won, 28-14. Their home opener against San Antonio (a 17-10 Fire victory) drew just 16,250, and the three other games at Legion Field hosted crowds of 11,187 (Birmingham 19, Barcelona 17), 9,764 (Birmingham 23, Montreal 16) and 15,186 (Birmingham 24, Orlando 23). Birmingham was 2-1-2 on the road in the regular season, losing to Sacramento (20-6) and San Antonio (17-14), defeating Frankfurt (17-7) and Ohio (27-24) and tying London (17-17). As was the case in their first season, the Fire was one and done in the postseason, losing to Orlando, 45-7, in the first round.

I confess, I didn't cover a single game, instead opting to stick to spring high school sports. When the Fire made it into the paper, it was via Associated Press wire reports. The only WLAF-related event I did show up for was when NFL Commissioner Paul Tagliabue visited Legion Field the week of Birmingham's home opener and held a short news conference. The gist of the visit was to let fans and city officials know that he loved Birmingham and that it was an integral part of the league – but that the city needed to be happy with the WLAF, because it wasn't going to get an NFL franchise. Well, he didn't come out and say it exactly like that, but he made it obvious that the city's "place" was in the developmental circuit and any future expansion of the big league would not include central Alabama. He also assured us all that the World League was stable. "We're very optimistic about it," Tagliabue said. "We've made our plans with the assumption that it's going to stay. After three years, hopefully, the league will be self-sustaining at the gate. We have every reason to believe it will be because of the increasing fan interest, player talent and communities the World League are located in. These are world-class cities that are ripe for pro sports."

As for my fandom – such as it was – that was confined to watching games on TV and even then, it was hardly appointment viewing. The Atlanta Braves, which had gone from worst to first in winning the National

League pennant in 1991, were playing great baseball again in 1992. Since Pop always had the TV on when Atlanta was playing, I opted to spend time with him watching Major League Baseball instead of spending money on minor league football. The good news is that the Fire had improved from a year earlier, finishing with a 7-3-1 record.

Still, my takeaway was that the club remained defined by a pedestrian offense, never scoring more than 28 points in a game. I didn't expect 50 a night, but a five touchdown showing every once in a while would've been nice, especially since Gailey's claim to fame was moving the ball and putting points on the board. As much as I had always prided myself on supporting Birmingham's professional teams, this was one I just never warmed up to. I could take or leave the Fire – and take or leave the WLAF as a whole. Turns out, I wasn't alone.

END OF THE ROAD

Two months after the Fire season ended, Maloof sold the franchise back to the league. Originally, the big story was who would take control of the franchise. But there was no need to find new owners, because on September 17, 1992, the NFL decided to deactivate the World League indefinitely, fold its North American franchises, and reboot it later as a European-based spring league. While the teams based overseas did well attendance-wise (Frankfurt led the league with 36,239 fans per game and Barcelona averaged more than 30,000 for its five home games), the interest stateside was underwhelming. While the Ohio Glory (which replaced the Raleigh-Durham franchise) averaged 30,892 per game, no other North American team did better than a 25,000 clip. And Birmingham, which had a reputation of being a rabid football town, was last in the league with 14,636 fans per game. From a minor league standpoint, those figures really aren't bad. But considering the NFL was trying push the league as a "major" developmental league – and travel costs were astronomical – it just stopped making sense to the bean counters. "If I had known this was going to be a two-year deal, I never would've taken the job," Gailey told the Montgomery Advertiser in October, 1992. "I thought with the NFL behind it, it would be something that would last. I guess I was wrong. The WLAF could be back, but it won't be back in Birmingham."

It's always sad to see teams and leagues falter – more than just players and coaches lose their jobs, so there are many people whose lives are adversely affected – but if America was looking for a spring league to take the place of the USFL, the WLAF simply wasn't it. Tagliabue said the NFL would "pause, re-orient and pursue an international strategy" when it came to its feeder league. Dallas Cowboys owner Jerry Jones, who voted to suspend the World League for a year, told Associated Press leaving North America behind was best for the circuit. "We've discussed that and think we can step up that operation," Jones said. "That was not a stumbling point at all. The interest in Europe is very impressive and our experience over the last two years tells us this is the direction to go."

EUROPEAN VACATION

In a technical sense, the WLAF lasted for 15 years – two as the World League of American Football, 12 as NFL Europe, and one as NFL Europa. But after its two seasons in the United States, it bolted America for good, restarting in 1995 with an all-European lineup. The "new" World League of American Football had six teams during the first year of its relaunch – reviving London, Barcelona and Frankfurt from the WLAF days and introducing the Amsterdam Admirals, Rhein Fire and Scottish Claymores. In 1998 the WLAF was rebranded as NFL Europe, and its lone season as NFL Europa was 2007, with five of its six franchises in Germany. Oddly enough, I wrote more stories about the Admirals than I ever did for Birmingham's team. Marcus Knight, who played college football at Michigan, was a high school standout at B.B. Comer High School in Sylacauga, which is a major part of The Daily Home's coverage area. I followed his lone season with the Admirals in 2003, and that allowed me to reacquaint myself with the circuit 13 years after it left the United States. The final game in league history was played on June 29, 2007 when the Hamburg Sea Devils defeated the Frankfurt Galaxy 37-28 in the World Bowl. Less than a week later, NFL commissioner Roger Goodell pulled the plug on the NFL's developmental league.

NFLE was never a money-maker, but losses up to $30 million per year (there were reports it lost $54 million in its final season) could no longer be ignored. Thus, the mother ship confined its international footprint to regular season and exhibition games involving actual NFL teams. In 2018, three NFL regular season games were played in London and one in Mexico City, and there are plans to continue to export games in the coming years. There has even been talk of placing an NFL franchise in London.

CANADIAN FOOTBALL LEAGUE

Birmingham's history with professional football was tied to upstart leagues with expiration dates – until 1995. That was the year the Magic City became part of the Canadian Football League, which was well-established long before any player was ever paid to play the gridiron game in Birmingham. Officially it was founded as the CFL in 1958, combining the Interprovincial Rugby Football Union and Western Interprovincial Football Union into one professional league. The first CFL season was split into the Interprovincial Rugby Football Union division, featuring the Hamilton Tiger-Cats, Montreal Alouettes, Ottawa Rough Riders and Toronto Argonauts, and the Western Interprovincial Football Union division, which was populated by the British Columbia Lions, Calgary Stampeders, Edmonton Eskimos, Saskatchewan Roughriders and Winnipeg Blue Bombers.

What separates the CFL from the rest of the tackle football world are rules unique to the north of the border game:

- The field is 110 yards long and 65 yards wide, and end zones are 20 yards deep.
- Teams have only three downs to make a first down, which makes the CFL much more of a passing game.
- Teams have 12 players on the field at once time – and extra receiver on offense, and additional defensive back on defense.
- It is possible to score a single point, called a rouge, via a kickoff, missed field goal attempt or punt. This point is awarded if a kick returner takes a knee in the end zone or runs out of bounds before advancing out of the end zone.
- Onside punts and field goals are possible. Any player lined up behind the punter or kicker can recover a kick as long as it travels at least 10 yards.
- All runners (except quarterbacks) and receivers are allowed in motion toward the line of scrimmage before the ball is snapped.
- There are no fair catches on punts; the returner must be given a five-yard cushion in order the field the kick.
- Defensive linemen must line up one yard off the line of scrimmage.
- Goal posts are located on the goal line.
- Point after attempts (converts) are attempted from the 32-yard line (with the line of scrimmage the 25). If a team opts to go for a two-point conversion, the line of scrimmage is the three-yard line.

- If a ball is fumbled out of bounds, it becomes the possession of the last team to touch it.
- The overtime procedure gives each team possession of the ball at the opponent's 35-yard line, and following a touchdown, a two-point conversion must be attempted. A maximum of two possessions for each team are allowed during regular season games. If no team has a lead after two tries, the game ends in a tie. In the postseason, however, the possessions continue until a winner is declared.

As far as its history goes, the CFL stuck with the same nine cities for its first 29 years, but dropped down to eight franchises in 1987 when the Montreal Alouettes folded. Actually, the first iteration of Alouettes went under in 1981 and were replaced by the Montreal Concordes, which were renamed the Alouettes again in 1986 but folded after the season. Montreal didn't have a CFL team again until 1996. The other original franchise to experience upheaval was the Rough Riders, which folded in 1996. The Rough Riders were replaced by the Renegades in 2002, but that club lasted only until 2005. The CFL team playing in Ottawa today is the Redblacks, founded in 2014. But the biggest change in the history of the CFL was the "American experiment."

Hoping to grab a piece of U.S. television money and expand its base, the CFL moved into the United States in 1993, adding the Sacramento Gold Miners to the league. This club was an expansion team, of course, but also a something of repackaged version of the WLAF's

Sacramento Surge since many of the same players and coaches were involved in the new venture.

"It's obvious that North America is going through a major economic restructuring and at the same time there are new business opportunities and the emergence of new trading partners," CFL Commissioner Larry Smith said during a November 12, 1992, news conference. "There is a real hunger for football in many cities that will never have NFL football, and at the same time there's an opportunity in my mind that we can sell a differential product." The hope was to add teams in San Antonio, Sacramento, Portland and Montreal for 1993, but only the Gold Miners made it in that season. In 1994 the league added three more U.S. based franchises – the Baltimore CFL Colts (later renamed the Stallions due to NFL "owning" the name Baltimore Colts), Las Vegas Posse and Shreveport Pirates. Baltimore was a rousing success – averaging close to 40,000 fans per home game – while the Pirates did relatively well at the box office, too. Las Vegas was a bust, folding after one season. Still, the CFL decided to continue to test American waters in 1995. That season, British Columbia, Calgary, Edmonton, Hamilton, Ottawa, Saskatchewan, Toronto and Winnipeg were part of the all-Canadian North Division, while the all-United States South Division included Baltimore, the Birmingham Barracudas, Memphis Mad Dogs, San Antonio Texans (relocated from Sacramento) and Shreveport.

The traditional CFL rules remained in place, although some of the American cities had to fudge a little because of stadium issues. Legion Field and the Liberty Bowl in Memphis, for example, were not configured to accommodate the 20-yard deep CFL end zones. Thus, when teams came to those stadiums, they played on a field that was 110-yards long and 65-yards wide, but had truncated end zones measuring 15-yards deep.

BIRMINGHAM BARRACUDAS (1995)

From a sports standpoint, Wednesday, January 11, 1995, is most notable for being the day the National Hockey League Players Association and owners agreed to end the NHL strike – one that had already wiped out almost three months of the 1994-95 season. As a hockey fan I was glad to hear it, but that was hardly the day's top headline. Not for me. In my sports world, the biggest news was Birmingham being granted a CFL franchise. "I was looking at putting a team in Orlando, San Antonio or Birmingham," new team owner Art Williams said at his introductory press conference. "But I attended Auburn University and this has always been like home for me. I believe the CFL is the next great thing happening in professional sports and we'll field a team that'll be unbelievable." Williams promised a more exciting brand of ball than the NFL. "It's not going to be like the Atlanta Falcons playing the New Orleans Saints – it's not gonna be that kind of crap," he boasted. "These kids are going to be out there pitching and catching. You'll be amazed." And as for the coach? "It'll blow your butt out of the water," Williams said, without naming said coach who would blow our butts out of the water. Yeah, the presser was a bit over the top but that was fine. Not only did it mean pro football was back in the Magic City, but it was back in an established league, and one that I absolutely loved. Even better, Memphis was also granted an expansion team for 1995, so the football rivalry between these cities would continue.

"This ain't the United States Football League and this ain't the World Football League," Williams boasted. "This is older than the NFL, and you've got an owner with a ton of money. Alabama is one of the best football states in America and it deserves to have professional football. "I'm making the necessary long-term commitment of my time and financial resources to make this franchise succeed."

When I was a kid, the local CBS affiliate would broadcast delayed (and truncated) CFL games on Sunday nights during the summer. That was my first introduction to the game, and I became a huge fan right from the start. I embraced the unique rules because they were different enough from those used in NFL and American college ball to make Canadian football special. I also liked the speed of the game and that there was a place for smaller, more mobile quarterbacks. Pop never could get used to the three downs to make a first down rule, and admitted that's what kept him from completely buying into the CFL. I tried to explain to him why the three-to-make-10 was actually a good thing (more of a sense of urgency for the offense), but he wouldn't budge on his opinion. We just agreed to disagree, as we often did. Fortunately, that didn't stop him from watching it with me, and I always got the impression he liked it more than he let on. I decided the Hamilton Tiger-Cats would be my favorite team (for no particular reason other than I liked the fact that the nickname was a combination of Tigers and Wildcats and I thought the black and yellow color scheme looked good), and scrounged the scoreboard page of the Birmingham News every Sunday hoping to find out how they fared. I never stopped following the league (NBC even showed a few games during the 1982 NFL strike), and once it dipped into the United States, I could actually watch the games on a regular basis thanks to ESPN2. So while it was always cool to know Birmingham would be part of a play for pay football organization, playing in the CFL might've just been the coolest thing yet for me. Simply put, while the Jets were my favorite pro football team, the CFL had become my favorite pro football league.

As I alluded to earlier, I always loved talking to Pop about sports – actually, I loved talking to him about everything. But this was the man who taught me how to do a baseball box score when I was barely old enough to read, and told me enough stories about baseball and football that I had a sense of the sports' tradition from the moment I began to follow them. Birmingham's entry in the CFL was certainly something I wanted to talk to him about, and I can remember thinking when I first found out I needed to call him and rag him about how wrong he was about the three-to-make-10 rule. But I couldn't. Pop died on Christmas Day, 1994, just three weeks after he was diagnosed with cancer. It was probably a full year before I stopped reaching for the phone to call him after a big game or when I heard big news. The fact that I couldn't do it anymore hurt like hell. I would've loved to have gone over coaching candidates and roster possibilities, and set up some kind of TV "play date" where he and I could get together the first time Birmingham played a game that was televised.

But that wasn't possible. Looking back, January 11, 1995, was one of the happiest sports days of my life because the CFL had decided to set up shop in my hometown. Not being able to share the joy with Pop, however, also made it one of the saddest.

PARDEE JOINS THE PARTY

Williams made millions of dollars as an insurance magnate, and supplemented his considerable income by writing books, conducting seminars and giving motivational speeches. Think Tony Robbins, buttermilk battered and Southern-fried. He was also a successful high school football coach in Georgia, winning a pair of "Coach of the Year" titles before trading in a whistle and clipboard for a suit and tie. But did the owner of Birmingham's latest pro football team know how to hire the right people to make this venture a success? It certainly seemed so. Roy Shivers was hired as general manager, and this was someone quite familiar with the CFL. He began his affiliation with the league in 1983 as an assistant coach with the B.C. Lions, and two years later became director of player personnel. During his tenure, he put together rosters that helped the Vancouver-based team participate in three Grey Cups and six Western Division finals. But then Williams was charged with hiring coaches, and he went big and bold.

Jack Pardee was named the head coach on Jan. 31 and John Jenkins, who put together relentless run-and-shoot attacks as both a head coach and offensive coordinator, was hired as OC.

My butt was not blown out of the water by the announcement, as Williams had promised, but my butt – and the rest of me – was pleased. "I'm not here as a stepping stone to somewhere else," Pardee said at his introductory news conference. "What I plan on doing is spending the rest of my coaching career here."

As far as I was concerned, both of those were major league hires. And Pardee brought a remarkable resume to the 'Cudas.

As a college player at Texas A&M, he was one of the "Junction Boys, and he went on to play 17 seasons in the NFL. But as a coach, he held top jobs in the NFL (Chicago, Washington and Houston), WFL (Florida), and USFL (Houston). Getting the CFL gig allowed him to hit for the cycle, making him the only man in history to serve as head coach in all four leagues. Although he was fired by the Houston Oilers after going 1-9 during the 1994 season, he led the team to the playoffs the previous four campaigns. His overall NFL record was 87-77. "The only reasons I'm here is the CFL has been around forever and because of the owner we have,"

Pardee told the Baltimore Sun. "In Art Williams, we have a guy who is not using mirrors. We're going to do it right or I wouldn't be here. I'm not trying to reinvent the wheel. I've always been a defensive guy. People ask why I got involved with the run-and-shoot. I say because it's hard to stop. The run-and-shoot kept me in this business the last 14 years. We're going to bring exciting football to Birmingham – football that's fun to play."

Jenkins had worked with Pardee at both the University of Houston and the USFL's Houston Gamblers. The Gamblers led the league in total offense and scoring in both 1984 and 1985, and his resume as OC at UH resulted in a butt load of offensive records. But Jenkins also had some CFL experience, spending time as a coach and scout for Winnipeg before following Pardee to Birmingham. "I want that run-and-shoot offense where we hurry up to the line with no huddle and look for a four or five-play series that results in scoring drives," Jenkins told the Star-Phoenix of Saskatchewan. "Our goal is to get 37 points every game, but I'll still take 10-7 wins over 50-48 losses." The rest of the staff included Greg Newhouse (defensive coordinator), Dan Brown (defensive line), Al Everest (special teams), Ronnie Vinklarek (offensive line), Brad Miller (conditioning), Jim Hilyer (volunteer coach) and Wes Cope (volunteer coach). On a personal level I was especially happy to see Hilyer become part of the Cudas. The "Father of UAB Football" was the school's first coach, leading the Blazers from Division III up to what is now known as the Football Championship Subdivision. As for making the adjustment from American to Canadian rules, Pardee wasn't worried. "Coaching's coaching," he told the Associated Press. "I don't see any problems. I like the league and I like the style of play."

STOCKING THE ROSTER

I had no quarrel with Shivers' efforts putting together a roster. Matt Dunigan was signed as the franchise quarterback on March 12, and that was a really big "get." Although he was 34 and had been dealing with injuries in recent seasons, he came to the 'Cudas as the CFL's second all-time leader in passing touchdowns (257), ranked third in passing yardage (37,221 yards) and fourth in completions (2,581). He had been in the CFL since 1983, and if there was any triggerman who could step in and step up for the expansion franchise, it was him. He would be the highest paid player in the league in 1995, pulling down $1.2 million in the first year of a three-year, $2.9 million deal he signed with Williams. Some solid insurance was added when Jimmy Klingler joined the team. Just two years removed from the University of Houston, he led the NCAA's top division in total offense (3,768 yards) and total touchdowns (32) during the 1992 season. Considering Dunigan's history with injuries, this was a great signing. Reggie Slack, a former Auburn quarterback, also inked a pact with the club to give the team three quality QBs. (He was traded to Winnipeg before Birmingham's regular season home opener, however). The roster featured a trio of former

Alabama players – offensive lineman Roosevelt Patterson, offensive tackle Thomas Rayam and wide receiver Prince Wimbley. But to succeed in the CFL you needed players who had already experienced CFL success, so Shivers brought in CFL defensive standouts Angelo Snipes, John Motton and Anthony Drawhorn. It was an impressive group of players and, along with the coaching staff, set the stage for what I hoped would be a memorable season at Legion Field.

UGH, BARRACUDAS?

March 14, 1995, is a day that will live in sports nickname infamy. That was the day Birmingham's CFL team was officially christened the "Barracudas." For two months, I had waited and wondered about the team's nickname, hoping it would be something dazzling. I don't recall if there were any rumors as to what it might be, and there was no name-the-team contest.

The WFL teams had tie-ins to the city (Americans saluted the All-America City while Vulcans paid tribute to the bare-butted God of the Forge that overlooked us); the USFL club reflected its owner (Stallions); and the WLAF representatives went outside the box (Fire) but still managed to be hip and colorful.

You could've run a million nicknames by me, though, and there's a good chance I would've picked any one of them before "Barracudas." Central Alabama brings to mind a lot of things, but a ferocious saltwater fish is not one of them.

Yet that's the name Williams picked, and the Georgia native (who graduated from Mississippi State and then earned his Master's degree at Auburn) had all the money, so he got to make all the rules. But why Barracudas? Did he once own a Plymouth Barracuda? Even if he did, most of them were confined to car shows by the mid-1990s. And before you point out the obvious, I know ... there aren't many lions in Detroit or bears in Chicago or giants in New York, either, but I give a pass to old school teams with old school nicknames. The people in charge of naming teams just didn't know any better back then. In the modern era, however, nicknames were designed to be a bit more relevant. Williams' explanation was this:

"It's an animal that's vicious and mean. No other team in pro sports is called the Barracudas. We even copyrighted the name to protect it. My wife and I went through the dictionary front to back and back to front looking for possibilities. When we finally began going through copyright searches, Barracudas really stood out." Stand out did it – like a sore thumb. If you haven't yet figured it out, I was terribly, terribly disappointed with the choice.

Williams said more than 400 other nicknames were considered, including Cougars, Bearcats, Bandits, Steel and Magicians. Sadly, they were not considered strongly enough. And when the logo was unveiled, I hated it, too. Team colors were teal, black, blue and orange, and the helmets were black, highlighted by a thin teal fish with an under bite. It actually made me miss the sick horse on

the Stallions' lids. But, Birmingham had a CFL team –
that was the important thing – and I decided to learn to
live with the stupid nickname because soon I would have
hats, tee shirts and pennants proclaiming my allegiance
to the Barracudas. P.S. The team was also known as the
"Cudas."

 That was not better. That was not better at all.

TRAINING CAMP

 The Barracudas held their training camp at Samford
University, and I was looking for any excuse I could find
to cover it. Fortunately, I had a legitimate reason when
David Gulledge tried out for the team. One of the
greatest quarterbacks in Jacksonville State University
history, he was also a former Pell City High School
standout who had been converted to defensive back.
And since Pell City was part of The Daily Home
coverage area, I decided to do some double and triple
dipping, talking to Gulledge about his prospects of
making the team and trying to find time to get in a few
words with coaches and players. I already had great
respect for Pardee based on his accomplishments in
football, and even more so after I was able to meet with
him following a practice. I was just another face in the
crowd when it came to sports writers, but he took the
time to answer all my questions thoughtfully, and I've
never forgotten that. "One thing about this league," I
remember him saying, "is that it's been around a long

time. It's stable, and when I had the chance to be a part of it, I jumped at it."

In fact, the staff and players were about as accommodating as any I've ever dealt with during my entire career. Dunigan was loaded with personality, and was genuinely excited about bringing CFL football to Birmingham. A Dallas native and graduate of Louisiana Tech University, he was glad the Canadian game had ventured into the Deep South and was confident Birmingham would not only accept the league but support it enthusiastically. The most vivid memory I have, though, is when I was driving out of the parking lot following a workout and Jenkins ran out in front of my car. Thanks to my cat-like reflexes, Birmingham's offensive coordinator lived to call another play.

By the way, Gulledge failed to make the team, but I was already invested that I was determined to cover them as much as possible. That would not be easy, since my primary duties involved high school and Alabama and Auburn football. And truth be told, if a news outlet had come along and offered me a chance to be the Barracudas' beat writer, I'd have jumped at the opportunity. Fortunately, the CFL season started earlier than the prep and college campaigns, so I was at least going to get in on the ground floor of the CFL's Alabama adventure. Professionally, I looked forward to it. Fan-wise, I was thrilled. After being burned by the other Birmingham teams, I was absolutely certain this one would last. Right?

LONGER, FASTER, WIDER

CFL seasons feature only two exhibition games, and both of Birmingham's were on the road. The team debuted with a 31-28 loss at Shreveport on June 16, and then fell hard to Baltimore, 37-0, on June 24 at a game played at the Orange Bowl. That exhibition was actually a marketing test for South Florida, which was angling to get a future CFL expansion team to be called the Miami Manatees. A crowd of just 13,000 showed up, but considering there was no "home" team involved that was probably as good as could be expected.

The preseason was all about working out kinks, so it didn't matter what Birmingham did in those tilts. What did matter was the regular season, and that began with a 38-10 road victory over Winnipeg on the Fourth of July. A team stocked with offensive stars played second fiddle to a defense that returned two Blue Bomber interceptions for touchdowns and forced six turnovers in all. The 'Cudas first TD was scored when Andre Strode picked off a Winnipeg pass and took it to the house. "When a defensive player does that, it kinda sets the tone for the night," Pardee told the Edmonton Journal. Dunigan was sidelined with an injured thumb but it made no difference. Klingler tossed a 96-yard TD pass for the winners' top offensive highlight as they pulled ahead 31-0 at the half. The game that billed itself as a "longer, wider, faster" version of the gridiron sport seemed to suit Birmingham just fine.

Just four days later the Barracudas traveled to Hamilton to face the Tiger-Cats, and this was where the fan in me was truly tested. I had been pulling for the Ti-Cats for two decades, but now that Birmingham had a franchise, I felt a moral obligation to the ray-finned fish that represented my hometown. It was almost like I was in a long-distance relationship with someone who lived in Canada, only to be swept off my feet by a paramour who moved in next door. But like the song says, "If you can't be with the one you love, love the one who was granted an expansion team in your city." I guess my decision to pull for Birmingham must've upset Hamilton, because the home team dominated the game, 31-10. Klingler again played long ball – this time with an 86-yard touchdown pass – and Marcus Grant closed the night with 182 receiving yards. But the defense that looked so good a week earlier was rocked by the Tiger-Cats defense, and Birmingham appeared to take a step back from Week One. Still, the 'Cudas split their season opening road trip, and through a scheduling quirk got a quick shot at revenge when Hamilton came to Legion Field on July 15.

HOMESTAND

Although I had to slip into my journalism britches for the showdown between the Barracudas and Tigers, I couldn't help but be excited as the CFL made its debut on Graymont Avenue.

Not only was I covering my first Canadian football game live, I was seeing my first one live and in person as well. And the fact that the team I had followed for years was going head-to-head against the one I had hoped to follow for many years to come was not lost on me, either. Regardless of the outcome, I just hoped this game would give me something good to write about. It did. Legion Field wasn't packed, but a crowd of 31,185 was quite good by Canadian standards. In fact, while it was below the debuts of the Americans and Fire, it exceeded that of the Stallions. And the game made a good first impression on those who decided to give the CFL a try. Grant continued to assert himself as one of the league's best wideouts and Dunigan had his Magic City coming out party in a 51-28 Barracudas victory. He threw a touchdown pass and ran for another in the first quarter, stopped long enough to a celebratory dance in front of the Hamilton bench, and went on to hurl two more TDs – one a 72-yard bomb to Grant. "A lot of people talked about how important this first (home) game was, but all I tried to do was go out and play some good football," Dunigan said. "The whole team played great and, honestly, the crowd really helped. The media and the front office has done a good job of educating the folks down here about the game, and it showed. Fans in Alabama know their football. Sure, we play a different brand of football than the NFL and the colleges, but it's still football. And if we play a good brand the fans will support us."

Pardee couldn't have asked for much more from his QB. "No doubt we play with more confidence when Matt's out there," he said. "He was a little rusty coming back from his (finger) injury, but it sure wasn't a bad performance. In our first two games, we made a lot of big plays. In this one, we made a few big plays and a lot of little ones, and Matt was responsible for much of that."

The "D" also returned to its thieving ways, and Fernando Thomas snagged an INT that he turned into a 41-yard touchdown to add insult to injury. Seven days before, Birmingham lost to this team by 21 points. On this night, they won by 23, which made for a jubilant locker room. Dunigan, as expected, was all smiles when it was over, and was especially pleased with the crowd. "Man, that was great," he said. "We looked up in the stands and saw what a huge crowd had come to see us, and we wanted to make sure we gave 'me our best effort and we did. That was fantastic."

My game story played up the offensive aspect of the win, as well as what appeared to be the huge step forward the 'Cudas had taken in becoming a team Birmingham would embrace: The fans seemed to love it. Birmingham owner Art Williams and head coach Jack Pardee surely did. And in a game that was billed as a make-or-break contest for the Magic City's latest entry into play-for-pay football, the Barracudas look like contenders. A 2-1 record three weeks into the season didn't promise anything, of course, but there was no reason to believe the future of the CFL in the Football Capital of the South wasn't a promising one. And the

'Cudas got to follow up their impressive home opener with two more home contests. The next club to come to town was the Saskatchewan Roughriders, and 25,321 patrons watched the 'Cudas go two-for-two in Birmingham. While the offense wasn't as explosive as it was a week early, another good defense performance made sure it didn't matter in a 24-14 win. Dunigan had a hand in all three major scores, hurling three touchdown passes. Unfortunately (for me) I missed this game since it was Talladega race week, and I was covering the Humminbird Fishfinder 500k Busch Series race. (In case you're wondering, Chad Little held off Jimmy Spencer to take the checkered flag at the "World's Fastest Speedway").

The three-game Magic City set ended on July 29, with 30,729 folks coming out to see the showdown between Birmingham and Baltimore. The Stallions were the crown jewel of U.S. expansion teams, having developed a great following from fans jilted by the Colts' midnight move to Indianapolis and succeeding on the playing field, as well. In 1994 the team made the Grey Cup (losing to BC), and was expected to be strong contenders for the CFL title in 1995. And while exhibition games are meaningless, the 'Cudas could still use their preseason game against the Stallions as motivation since they were beaten by 37 points and shutout. I had to miss this one as well, as I was knee deep in putting together our high school and college football special sections at The Daily Home. Still, I had the game on the radio at the office and hoped the

Barracudas could continue their winning ways. They could not. This game was never a contest, as Baltimore smothered the hosts, 36-8. The Birmingham offense was limited to 150 yards of total offense while Baltimore, through Tracy Ham's passing and Mike Pringle's rushing, had their way against an overmatched defense. "Baltimore is a great team and we made them look even better than they are," Pardee told the Calgary Herald. "We didn't play anywhere near the level we have to in order to win." Still, Birmingham was 3-2, and with 13 regular season games to go, Magic City fans would have plenty of opportunities to see the team win again. Most of them took a pass.

HERE WE GO AGAIN

There was always the fear that the CFL might be a bit of a hard sell in Birmingham, and that college football (and even the NFL) would potentially have a negative impact on attendance once all the seasons were in progress. I knew it would affect my attendance – even in the press box – since my job would be taking me to Bryant-Denny Stadium and Jordan-Hare Stadium most Saturdays and I was also required to work in the office when I wasn't at games. The home opener would be the only game I got to see in person, which was a bummer considering how hyped I was about covering the CFL. What I didn't expect, however, was the mass abandonment of the 'Cudas by area gridiron fans. Birmingham followed up the home loss to Baltimore with a 30-23 road setback to BC, and played next at Legion Field on Saturday, Aug. 12 – still before the college season was under way. A 50-24 victory over Winnipeg was witnessed by just 17, 328 fans. The 'Cudas' final game before having to share the stage with more "traditional" football came on Aug. 26. They lost to Calgary, 37-14, the team they had beaten 31-28 eight days before. This time, 19,652 fans were at Legion Field to watch Calgary sub Jeff Garcia pick apart the hosts. "We made Garcia look like the all-time best one who's ever played the game," Pardee told the Anniston Star. "But he is a good one."

Sadly – and ultimately devastating for the franchise – that marked the final time the Barracudas drew anywhere near that many fans. In fact, they never even came close to hitting the 10,000 mark the rest of the way. After finishing the first half of the regular season 5-4, they duplicated that record over the second half. Results, in order, were a 56-46 win at Ottawa, 28-20 loss at Baltimore, 40-9 win vs. Ottawa, 28-19 loss at Memphis, 34-20 win vs. Shreveport, 38-28 win vs. San Antonio, 29-28 win at Shreveport, 45-18 loss vs. Edmonton (a game that saw Dunigan break the same finger he injured during training camp), and 48-42 loss at San Antonio.

The season ended with a 52-9 drubbing at the hands of the Texans and a 10-9 record. It also effectively ended the Barracudas. Williams announced after the game that, "the only thing that's certain is we won't be back in Birmingham in the CFL in the fall."

While the team itself was all over the map in wins and losses fans had long stopped caring before the season came to an end. I was still very much into it: Dunigan, Jason Phillips, Grant and Anthony Drawhorn had seasons that would land them on the CFL Southern Division all-star team, and Dunigan finished with 4,910 passing yards and 34 TDs. Win or lose I was paying close attention, but that meant I couldn't ignore the fact that fans were ignoring the team in a major way. Birmingham's final home game was played Thursday, October 19, against Edmonton, with 8,910 fans watching. On the bright side, that was more than showed up for the victory over San Antonio on Sunday, October 8. The number of ticket-buying customers for that one totaled 6,859 – still 545 more than attended the conquest of Shreveport on Sunday, October 1. "As a coach, the biggest thing you can do to impact attendance and interest is to win football games," Pardee told the Associated Press in September. "We're in the thick of a playoff hunt right now, and we need to win games whether we're in front of 100 people or 100,000."

Williams thought – and the thought made perfect sense to me – that Birmingham's best option was to play on Sundays to avoid going up against Alabama and Auburn. As much as I enjoyed the NFL, I much preferred to watch Birmingham's pro football team play. I assumed there were at least 25,000 other people who felt the same way I did, and would pay a visit to Graymont Avenue on the Sundays when the 'Cudas were in town. But the sad truth is that the novelty of

Canadian football wore off once American football started up. And on Sundays, local fans were apparently content to sit at home and watch the Falcons or Saints or whatever NFL game was beaming into their living rooms. Williams had already set the stage for the team's demise when, during the middle of the season, he started talking about how much money the team was losing. "The CFL is coming across to the public as minor league football," Williams said. "And we have major league expenses."

There was talk among some of the American-based owners of pulling the U.S. teams out of the league and forming a new spring league. Even while the season was under way they had hinted that the CFL needed to shift more toward NFL-style rules to appeal to American fans. My first preference is to get a contract with CBS, sign a few marquee players and play in the spring at Legion Field." A USFL-type reboot would've been nice, I suppose, but I was fully on board with the CFL. I wanted "my" franchise to stay put and keep playing that longer, faster, wider stuff. My belief was that the teams in the United States needed to adapt to the Canadian game and the CFL should never, ever alter its rules to appease owners who believed otherwise. Instead, the Birmingham Barracudas were one and done, adding their name and logo to Birmingham's pro sports graveyard.

And as much as I hated to see the WFL and USFL teams fold, I think this failure hit me harder than them all. I might've hated the nickname, but I loved the team and the league. Even though I was a grown man who was well aware of Birmingham's pro football history, I believed the CFL was in the United States to stay, and Birmingham would always be a part of it. A circuit that featured unique rules and had U.S. teams in non-NFL cities seemed like a winning combination for a second pro football league in North America. I'm the first to admit that my rosy outlook was colored by the fact that I was a vocal proponent of that whole Canadian-style philosophy. I make no apologies for being a CFL fanboy then, and I remain one now. The New York Jets might be my favorite professional team, but the CFL is my favorite professional league. That being said, the Tiger-Cats and I worked through things after my one-year affair with the 'Cudas. That was a difficult time for both of us, but over the years it's made our bond even stronger.

CFL: ALIVE AND (RELATIVELY) WELL

By the time the CFL took the field again in 1996, the "American experiment" had completely collapsed. The CFL's Board of Governors met in February of that year and decided to make their league all-Canadian once again. And it would stay very much Canadian. As the U.S.-based teams started dying off Memphis Coach Pepper Rogers said the CFL should changes its name and adopt four downs. Smith shot that idea down quickly. "We're going to make zero rule changes to this league unless we have partners who have made a long-term commitment to this league and the future of this league, and even at that point it has to be beneficial to the league," the commissioner told the Star-Phoenix. "The rule changes are a non-issue. Why make rule changes if people try to leverage the league for their own purposes, if we don't have long term partners? We are the CFL. We have a brand of football we're selling. This is our brand. This is our style."

Although Baltimore was an extremely strong franchise with great ownership, the NFL was returning to Maryland's largest city in 1996, and that doomed the Stallions. Ironically, Baltimore was the CFL's best team in 1995, winning the Grey Cup, finishing 18-3 (with a 13-game winning streak to end the year), and leading the league in attendance. When they took the field the next season, they were the Montreal Alouettes. Shreveport and Memphis folded, and a bid to relocate the 'Cudas to Shreveport failed, officially ending Birmingham's tenure in the league. The remnants of the Barracudas were picked up by Shreveport businessman Boyd Parker, who said he was ready to present a deal to the CFL that would keep Dunigan with the team and give the "Bayou Barracudas" a hometown hero to cheer for in '96. That, of course, didn't happen. The last American franchise to go out of business was San Antonio.

A (very) small consolation prize for me was that Dunigan signed with Hamilton for 1996. That meant I could continue to cheer for the QB I rooted for in Birmingham since he had joined the team I called my "own" before the 'Cudas. When the CFL resumed that season, it looked very much like the CFL of old – nine teams and two divisions.

And that's where the CFL stands today. The only difference is the team in Ottawa is now called the Redblacks, and there is talk of adding an expansion team to Halifax, Nova Scotia. Unlike every other football league Birmingham has been a part of, this one plays on, marching to the beat of its own drummer and maintaining its unique identity. But I still miss the 'Cudas. It was the one franchise I truly thought would last.

XFL

The brainchild of Vince McMahon, the XFL (that was its official name ... calling it the Extreme Football League would get you slapped) blew in with all the bombast you'd expect from a world champion heel – and exited like the no-name baby face he pummeled within the first minute of action. Does that analogy work? I don't know because – except for one summer when I was 10 and my mother's friend took me and her kid to Boutwell Auditorium (the local 5,000-seat sports and concert arena) to watch Monday night rasslin' – I never followed it. Predetermined athletic events were just not my thing, so when I learned the world's most successful wrestling promoter was getting in the football business, I was highly skeptical. McMahon had turned World Wrestling Entertainment into a juggernaut, and the man knew how to make money. Having a knack for making hundred dollar bills multiply is quite helpful when starting a new sports venture. Still, I couldn't help but wonder if his experience in over-the-top theatrics would be a hindrance instead of a help when it came to football.

McMahon held a news conference on Feb. 3, 2000, announcing that exactly a year later the XFL would open its inaugural season. "The appetite for professional football continues long past the Super Bowl," McMahon said. "The XFL is more than just an extension of the football season, it is a completely new product that not only fills a void for football fans, but will give the casual fan an all-access pass to a football experience unlike any other to date. The action will feature the best football players available and will be highly competitive, hard-hitting, and most importantly, fan friendly. Guaranteed." And brother, this was going to be manly football played by manly men. Forget about that silly ol' pansy stuff you got from the NFL (and the world's most elite tackle football players). "This will not be a league for pantywaists or sissies," McMahon said. "This won't be an overregulated, antiseptic brand of football. The XFL will take you places where the NFL is afraid to go because, quite frankly, we are not afraid of anything."

The XFL – working in a single entity structure – was made up of eight teams divided into two divisions. The Birmingham Thunderbolts, Chicago Enforcers, New York/New Jersey Hitmen and Orlando Rage played in the East, while the Las Vegas Outlaws, Los Angeles Extreme, Memphis Maniax and San Francisco Demons were in the West. The regular season lasted 10 weeks with the top two teams from each division advancing to the playoffs. The teams consisted of a 38-man active roster and seven-man reserve team and the pay was "real world" decent; Quarterbacks received $50,000 for the season, kickers $35,000 and the rest of the players around $45,000. Each regular season game also featured a $100,000 bonus pool divided equally among players on the winning team. Of course TV, as always, is key, and NBC was the flagship network.

Hooking up with a major broadcast partner was a huge early win for the league, and it also had cable deals with UPN and TNN. The main game would be shown each Saturday night on NBC as a lead-in to "Saturday Night Live." The TV presentation was billed as "all-access," with players and coaches wired for sight and sound on the field, sidelines and locker rooms. "The XFL will attract the entire football-viewing demographic, strengthened by our unique understanding of the young, adult male audience," McMahon said. "That, combined with our extensive experience filling venues and executing live events will help lead to the success of the XFL." The league's rule innovations combined elements from college football and the CFL, and threw in some of its own creations. For the most part, I liked them.

- The extra point kick was eliminated. Following a touchdown, the offense attempted a 1-point conversion via a run or pass. Also, the defense could return a fumble or interception for a single point.
- There were no fair catches on punts; the returner was given a 5-yard cushion to field the ball. The kicking team could not cross the line of scrimmage until the ball was kicked, and after it traveled 25

yards it was considered live and could be covered by either team.

- One man was allowed in motion toward the line of scrimmage as long as he lined up outside the tackles.
- A receiver needed only one foot in bounds for a reception.
- There was no coin toss. Instead, one player from each team lined up side-by-side on one of the 30-yard lines, with the ball placed at the 50. At the sound of the ref's whistle, the two players ran toward the ball and whoever gained possession could choose to kick or defer.
- Teams had 35 seconds to get a play off after the clock is stopped following a dead ball and 25 seconds after any clock stoppage.
- Kickoffs had to be returned from the end zone unless the kick went out of the end zone.
- Defensive players were allowed to use the "bump and run" on offensive players down field.
- The overtime procedure gave each team a possession at the opponents' 20-yard line with no first downs possible. If Team A scored a touchdown in less than four downs, Team B would have to score the same number of downs or less to keep the game going. No field goals were allowed until fourth down but if Team A failed to score on its opening O.T. possession, Team B could waive the first three downs of its possession and try a field goal to win the game.

BIRMINGHAM THUNDERBOLTS (2001)

By May, 2000, Birmingham was already in the mix for an XFL franchise and by June, negotiations with the city had gotten serious. As is the case any time I hear "new" football might be in the offing, I'm interested, and the financial structure of the XFL appeared to be sound. But was I excited?

Well, I was closing in my 40th year on planet earth. Having been burned so many times before, I don't think I was capable of getting "excited" about Brand X football any more. And McMahon's bluster was already a turnoff, so I wasn't inclined to go all-in. But, I was still going to give it every chance to win my heart and mind. Hopefully, the wrestling influence would be minimal and once the whistle blew, the football would be the main attraction. Birmingham's latest pro football venture was made official on Aug. 1, 2000, when McMahon held a news conference at The Club. Joining him was his daughter, Stephanie McMahon, other XFL officials, and Birmingham dignitaries. Gerry DiNardo, who had most recently led the fortunes of LSU, was introduced as head coach. I considered this a good step forward. While DiNardo had never coached pro ball and was just 59-76-1 in college stints at Vanderbilt and LSU, it was still a "name" hire. "If you can't enjoy coaching where people are so passionate about football, then you can't enjoy coaching," DiNardo said. "Some may view coaching where fans are so knowledgeable as a challenge, but I view it as a positive to be in a market where people really care about the game of football."

As for McMahon, he insisted Birmingham and the XFL had a bright future together. "I thrive on challenges and thrive on people doubting whether we can do certain things," McMahon said. "I would suggest that Birmingham has never failed in terms of football, it's been the pro leagues that have failed Birmingham. This league is not going to fail Birmingham. It has too much going for it. We know what we're up against, and carrying the burden of prior leagues that have failed. This type of football is different than other football that has been here. We're not looking for this to be a flash in the pan. We're looking to carve out a niche, and we certainly will." I was covering the event for The Daily Home, and was a bit surprised by the excitement among some of my fellow (younger) sports writers. They seemed truly optimistic about the league and the team, citing the NBC deal as giving it "major league" status.

Certainly that was a plus, but just because something's on television doesn't mean it will be successful. TV shows get canceled all the time, and McMahon was making it quite clear the XFL was very much a made-for-TV league. And NBC – which has been priced out of the last NFL television negotiations – had to produce something spectacular to keep Neilson families at home on Saturday evenings. The trick was selling a brand of football that wasn't NFL-caliber. The money was good for minor league football, but it was still minor league football. That being the case, a better plan of attack might have been promoting the league as a showcase for the stars of the future. McMahon wanted none of that. He was trying to make the XFL out to be competitors of the NFL, and frankly, that was ridiculous. This would be a circuit stocked with some players hoping to get a shot at the big leagues and others who never had a realistic shot to begin with.

And yes, I was jaded. Having lived through the rise and fall of the WFL, USFL, WLAF and CFL (in Birmingham), I had come to expect the worst when it came to pro football played under the shadow of Vulcan. I wanted it to last, but then again, I had wanted all of my hometown's teams to last (although, as previously noted, the Fire left me mostly cold). Fact is, none of the teams lasted. But, there was no harm in giving this new one a chance. What did I have to lose (except another team to root for)?

BRINGING THE THUNDER (BOLTS)

Birmingham was supposed to reveal its nickname and colors on August 24, 2000, but two days before the big reveal, news broke that the XFLers would be known as the Birmingham Blast.

When I heard about it I remember thinking, "Uh, that might not be such a good idea." I wasn't the only one who had reservations. Not only had there been the tragic 16th Street Baptist Church bombing in the 1960s, but more than 40 bombs had been detonated in the city dating back to the 1940s, almost all relating to the civil rights movement.   There was also a bomb blast that killed an off-duty police officer at the New Woman, All Women Health Care Clinic on Southside in 1998. While associating "Blast" with those events might've been a stretch to those whose only focus was cool nicknames, it wasn't worth the backlash. So, team officials made an 11th hour decision to change the name to "Thunderbolts," which was quickly shortened to "Bolts." The colors were purple, yellow and silver, and the white helmets featured a purple "B" just above the top center of the facemask with seven yellow bolts of lightning (with purple and silver trim) shooting out from it and spreading out over the rest of the helmet. I thought the hats looked great and the purple jerseys and white pants were quite stylish, too.

And since all the XFL nicknames were going for the hip and edgy vibe, I had no issue with the Bolts at all. So far, so good.

MAKING THE TEAM

In October, 2000, a two-phase draft was held for the XFL's eight teams. In the first phase, clubs selected up to 11 territorial players from their three designated colleges. In the case of the Bolts, those schools were Alabama, Auburn and UAB. In the second phase, teams drafted from a central talent pool put together by the league, and could bring 70 players to training camp. After that they could go after players via the free agent route or through trades (there was also a supplemental draft in December), but had to have the roster whittled down to 45 by opening day. And since opening day was the first weekend in February, that meant there was very little time to put a team together and have them ready to play. Or ready to play well. Birmingham's most high-profile signing came in January when the Bolts inked a pact with Jay Barker, who quarterbacked Alabama to the 1992 national championship and prepped at Hewitt-Trussville High School. Barker came to the XFL after spending three years with the CFL's Toronto Argonauts, and his pedigree as a hometown football hero was unquestioned. "Just to have the chance to play again at Legion Field is exciting ... I don't think I've ever lost a game there," Barker said. "It's also going to be great to play at home in front of friends and family. At first I was a little skeptical about the XFL, about whether it would be legitimate football because of the ties to the WWE. But (Bolts general manager) Tim

Berryman and Coach DiNardo made me feel comfortable and assured me that the football is real." If you can't afford superstars you need to go after familiar (former) stars, so this was a signing that most certainly garnered local interest.

By the time the roster was cut down to 45, the Bolts featured nine players from its three territorial schools, including former Auburn running back James Bostic. As for Barker, he was relegated to backup duties in the beginning since Casey Weldon was signed as the starting QB. While running Florida State's potent attack, Weldon was Heisman Trophy runner-up in 1991.

I certainly couldn't complain about Birmingham's options behind center. And when I eyeballed the entire roster, it was apparent that many of Birmingham's players were past their prime. That was OK, though; this could still be fun if done right.

My quarrel with the Fire wasn't that they were not major league, only that they played the most boring brand of football I'd ever seen up to that point. As long as you put on a good show, I'll be happy. As was the case with the Fire and the Barracudas, my first XFL game would be in a working capacity as Birmingham hosted Memphis at Legion Field on Sunday, Feb. 4. "We feel like we'll be able to move the football pretty well," Weldon said during media day. "(Wideout Stepfret) Williams is a really quiet guy, but he's also one of those people who'll go out there and work hard and make things happen. But really, I think all the guys on our team are that way. We realize XFL games are going to be a big production with the cameras and microphones, but we also know it's our job to play football and win games. We want to start the trends Sunday against Memphis, and we want to score a lot of points."

To prep for the game, I decided to watch the XFL's first NBC broadcast the night before – New York/New Jersey at Las Vegas. Not to be overly dramatic, but that game came dangerously close to completely killing my interest in the league.

WELL, THAT WAS AWFUL

Remember how I said I wasn't a rasslin' fan and worried that the XFL would give off too much of a rasslin' vibe? Its TV debut most certainly did. It was a WWE telecast minus the in-ring competition. Opening night featured a boring game, won by Las Vegas, 19-0. But first games in new leagues aren't always spectacular, so that didn't really trouble me. And players got to put nicknames on the back of their jerseys like "He Hate Me," which seemed silly but, again, no biggie. The problem was that the contest was wrapped in some really embarrassing trappings. From the telecast's opening – where "The Rock" extolled the virtues of the league in his full Rock persona, to a promo with "Stone Cold" Steve Austin, also in character, insulting the NFL – this had "joke" written all over it. And it wasn't funny. Throw in a staged flirtation between a quarterback and a cheerleader in the locker room, and it all just seemed sleazy. While the production values were first-rate – this was hardly NBC's first rodeo in sports – it was as though the event was geared toward horny 15-year old boys. If this was what McMahon was selling, I wasn't interested in buying. My opinion had already been shaped, and I wasn't sure what the Bolts could do to change it.

THIS LEAGUE IS NOT FOR ME

I didn't have to cover this game for The Daily Home ... I could've taken the day off and let Associated Press handle it. But I wanted to see it in person and find out if maybe it could possibly bring out the fan in me. It really didn't. There were all sorts of in-stadium activities to make the game interactive, and a lot of time and effort went into making live XFL games an experience. You have to give McMahon and his people credit for delivering on the spectacle. But I never got beyond the fact that this was a WWE production, and that turned me off. It appeared much more effort had been put into the production than the actual product. I'm a football fan, and when I go to the stadium, I'm there for the football.

A crowd of 35,321 showed up to see the Maniax beat the Bolts, 24-22, in a game that saw the visitors race out to a 19-0 lead before the home team rallied. Weldon struggled for much of the day, and fans wanted to see Barker behind center. "The boos didn't affect me," Weldon said. "I went out and played much better after they started booing. But I knew they wanted Jay in there. It's his hometown." DiNardo laughed off the

quarterback "controversy." "We weren't looking good at
the time, and when the fans boo it's either the coach or
the quarterback," he said. "I was glad they picked on
Casey instead of me." He did promise if the fans stuck
with the team, they'd give them a reason to cheer. "The
crowd was great," DiNardo said. "We certainly wanted
to win for them, but hopefully what they saw will bring
them back."

The teams had limited training camp work and there
were no exhibitions, so this contest was as sloppy as you
might expect.

Again, no big deal; anyone expecting newly
assembled teams to be in midseason form in the first
game of their first season were expecting far too much. I
remember writing a column after the first couple of
games saying I would withhold judgment on the league
for a few more weeks, giving it time to grow – and grow
on me. I watched the next week's game – a 19-14 road
win over New York/New Jersey – and simply tried to
avoid the distractions of the WWE-style announcers.
Once again the play was sloppy, and I lamented the lack
of offense. On February 18 the Bolts returned home to
face the Enforcers, winning 14-3 in a game was 7-3 until
Birmingham closed it out with a 95-yard interception
return for a score. As hard as I tried, I just couldn't stay
interested. When the season hit the halfway point, I had
already admitted – in print – that this team and this
league wasn't for me. And as it turned out, Birmingham's
back-to-back wins in the second and third weeks were
the only ones they registered. The Bolts lost their final

seven games, falling to Orlando (30-6), San Francisco (39-10), Los Angeles (35-26), Las Vegas (34-12), Chicago (13-0), Orlando (29-24), and New York/New Jersey (22-0). Oh, I wrote about the team throughout its 2-8 season, attending several practices and press conferences. That was part of my job, and I tried to help people who were interested keep track of what was going on. As a fan, though, I just didn't care.

The TV broadcasts were so over the top and ridiculous I bailed on watching telecasts than didn't involve the Bolts, and the best part of Birmingham games – for me – was that they eventually ended and I could switch the channel and start watching basketball. The Thunderbolts finished 1-4 at Legion Field, with their last home game (against the Hitmen) drawing 10,749 fans. A week before in a loss to the Rage, 10,163 people came to Graymont Avenue to watch. By the end of the year, Birmingham was next to last in XFL attendance, averaging 17,002 fans per game (Chicago pulled just 15,710 for games at Soldier Field). Of all the professional teams that had called Birmingham home, this one was – by most standards of measurement – the biggest bust.

XFL GOES OUT LIKE A LAMB

After pulling excellent television ratings for its opening game, XFL telecasts went into rapid decline. In fact, ratings hit record lows as the season progressed – an embarrassment for both McMahon and NBC. Still, knowing all the money that was invested, I had no idea that the league was in trouble. I figured I'd have to start paying attention to it again when camp opened later in the winter, and that point I'd try to psyche myself up enough to write about it. Turns out, there was no upcoming training camp. On May 10, less than two months after Los Angeles defeated San Francisco, 38-6, in the XFL championship game, the league folded. NBC didn't want to continue bleeding dollars for a league few people were watching, and McMahon is a smart enough business person to realize it was a losing proposition. "We tried to figure out every conceivable way to make this work," McMahon said. "But we came to the cold, hard decision that this was not going to work."

Many XFL proponents blamed negative media coverage as a major contributor to the league's demise. However, as someone who was in the media as the time and, as a fan, a longtime supporter of NFL alternatives, the ultimate blame rests with the XFL. Teams had barely a month to train, and with no preseason games and a 10-game season, clubs didn't mesh until they had almost run out of games. And the telecasts, which featured loudmouth announcers trying to generate controversy and drag coaches into their shtick, were less about football and more about showmanship. This particular mash-up of sports and entertainment was a miscalculation.

The cartoonish, larger than life world of wrestling is a very different "TV show" than professional football.

While there's no doubt there can be a demographic crossover, neither fans of football nor fans of wrestling got what they wanted. As is always the case, I was sad to see people lose their jobs. The league bored me, but I don't ever want to see honest endeavors fail, either. The going out of business news conference was a sad one, and I think those who worked for the league were genuinely stunned that it didn't get at least another year. The Bolts front office staff was first-rate from top to bottom, and the XFL certainly didn't fail because of their efforts. But fail it did, and from a strictly personal standpoint, I wasn't going to miss it. As a fan, I had written it off long before McMahon gave the "do not resuscitate" order. "When the league was in freefall, we knew NBC was going to pull out," Bolts general manager Tim Berryman said. "We knew this was a risky deal. But I'm sure Birmingham will get another shot at pro football down the road."

Of course I am a collector of all things related to Birmingham, so I already had tee shirts and caps related to the Bolts. At the first press conference, they even handed out mesh XFL jerseys, and I still have one tucked away in storage. I scored really big about a month after the league folded, though. I stopped by a sporting goods store to get some golf balls, and noticed a rack of XFL gear marked down dramatically. Team baseball caps were only $2, and the official Spalding XFL game ball (it was black with red stripes), was only $18, marked down from $75. I bought the ball and eight caps (representing all eight teams). For someone who wasn't overly enthused by the XFL or Bolts, you'd never know it by looking at my Fan Cave; aside from the caps and game ball, I also have a complete set of micro helmets representing all eight teams.

Oh, and for those who actually liked the XFL, a new and improved version (seriously, it was much improved) took the field in 2020: Faster, with more plays, fewer interruptions and zero gimmicks. We're sifting through all the recommendations we've received to improve the game, whether they've come from fans like you, or those who've devoted their lives to this sport. Bottom line: every element of the game is under review to see where improvements should be made, and we plan to field-test each potential change before accepting it as a component of the new XFL. Players earn roughly \$7,500 per game, although those designated as "marquee players" (especially quarterbacks) are paid a much higher salary annually. Contracts are for one year. Taking the field in the inaugural season of the rebooted XFL were the Dallas Renegades, DC Defenders, Houston Roughnecks, Los Angeles Wildcats, New York Guardians, Seattle Dragons, St. Louis BattleHawks and Tampa Bay Vipers.

The league made it through half of its regular season before it was forced (along with virtually every other sports competition) to suspend operations due to the COVID-19 virus. By late April all of its employees were laid off, the league filed for bankruptcy, and the second version of the XFL was no more.

ALLIANCE OF AMERICAN FOOTBALL

Seventeen years after Birmingham last had pro football, it found itself back in the game thanks to the Alliance of American Football – an eight-team, single entity spring league founded by Charlie Ebersol. Like all the leagues that came before it, it promised to be built to last: "Led by some of the most respected football minds in the game, The Alliance of American Football is high-quality professional football fueled by a dynamic Alliance between players, fans and the game. Fans will be able to stream Alliance matchups live via the free Alliance app while accessing integrated fantasy options with real rewards — for themselves and the players they are cheering on. Players will have state-of-the-art protection on the field and ample opportunities off it. The Alliance will provide players a comprehensive bonus system, post-football career planning as well as counseling and scholarship support for postsecondary education. Founded by TV and film producer Charlie Ebersol and Hall of Famer Bill Polian, The Alliance features eight teams, under a single entity structure, playing a 12-week season kicking-off February 9, 2019 on CBS and culminating with the championship game the weekend of April 26-28, 2019." Ebersol's father, Dick, teamed with McMahon to create the original XFL, so the "guilt by association" aspect caused me to view the new league with heavy skepticism. However, the Alliance got off to an impressive start by signing big name coaches like Steve Spurrier and Dennis Erickson and putting in place some experimental rules that I really liked:

- Only two-point conversions are allowed after each touchdown; there are no PAT kicks.
- There are no kickoffs. Halves and post-score possessions begin on each team's own 25-yard line, the same as touchbacks in the NFL and NCAA. In lieu of an onside kick, a team can keep possession of the ball by attempting an "onside conversion" play from its own 28-yard line and gaining at least 12 yards.
- The play clock runs only 30 seconds, 10 seconds shorter than in the NFL.
- Teams have 50 players on each roster, with some selected by a territorial draft. The territory assigned to a team consists of at least five colleges plus designated professional teams.
- Only one quarterback can be taken from a team's region. A quarterbacks-only "Protect or Pick" draft was held in November so teams could sign their allocated quarterback or go after an unprotected QB.

- Two coach's challenges per team are the only replays; no challenges in last two minutes of either half or any overtime period are allowed.
- No games can end in ties.
- A "sky judge" is an extra official in the press box who has final say on rulings.

The league also made it very clear they hoped their players would be able to use the AAF as a springboard to the NFL. While the original XFL immediately tried to antagonize Goliath, this circuit stressed harmony from the beginning, keeping its slingshot safely tucked away. And the money wasn't bad at all; players got three-year, non-guaranteed contracts worth $250,000, and could freely jump to the NFL at the end of any given season.

The Atlanta Legends, Arizona Hotshots, Birmingham Iron, Memphis Express, Orlando Apollos, Salt Lake Stallions, San Antonio Commanders and San Diego Fleet were the inaugural franchises and the league had TV contracts with CBS, the CBS Sports Network, NFL Network, TNT and BR/Live in 2019. One thing that jumped out at me were the number of "secondary" markets in the Alliance. Only Atlanta and Arizona (Tempe, to be precise) were in current NFL markets. The league's rollout was impressive; everything from the Alliance website to its viral promotions seemed to be first-class, and the closer it got to the start of the season, the more excited I got.

BIRMINGHAM IRON (2019)

The Iron was scheduled to debut on the second Sunday of February in 2019, and that meant I had to buy caps and tee shirts and all the keepsakes I could afford because when I hear the words "pro" and "football" and "Birmingham," that means someone is about to get my money. And I also like to get a head start on gathering memorabilia. Morbid, perhaps, but when you've seen as many teams die as I have, you want to get all the tokens of remembrance as you can while there's still time. And I knew the Alliance would have a limited time because all American-based professional football leagues not carrying the NFL acronym have expiration dates. The season opener came on February 10 when the Iron hosted the Memphis Express.

What was very different about this debut is that for the first time in my life making a trip to Legion Field was a bit of a chore because I no longer lived in or near Birmingham. In 2006, I landed a sports writing job that took me from the Cotton State to the Palmetto State. And by the time the AAF debuted, I had already worked at two different newspapers in the Upstate of South

Carolina and was now running my own website, adamsonmedia.com. One of the focal points of the site is "alternative football," and the Alliance fit the bill.

So on opening day I traveled from Greenville, South Carolina (where I now live) and got credentials for the game in order to gather up information for this book and do a game story for my website. I realized on the drive down that not only had I been to Legion Field for every home opener in every professional football league Birmingham had been in, but I had seen all of the home games against Memphis teams. It also occurred to me that this was the first time I had been in Legion Field's press box in 14 years. It was worth it. Birmingham won the game, 26-0, but the Iron also won me over as a fan again. Remember, by the time the XFL Bolts went out of business I had zero interest in them, and had no idea how I'd react to yet another secondary league. Perhaps it was a case of being overcome with nostalgia – and maybe even being a bit homesick – but I loved it. I didn't care that it wasn't NFL, USFL, CFL or WFL level, it was still my old city playing in a new league and it made me feel young again.

Iron quarterback Luis Perez - who frankly I'd never heard of until the team signed him - became one of my new favorite players after going 19-33-0 passing for 252 yards. Throw in four Nick Novak field goals and two fourth quarter touchdown scampers by former Alabama star Trent Richardson, and the hosts gave most of the 17,039 fans at Legion Field - and me - a happy ending. The Iron netted 327 yards of total offense, and although only 86 came on the ground, they were enough to wear the Express down. Outside linebacker Jonathan Massaquoi was in on seven tackles and had two sacks, while Beniquez Brown also had seven takedowns and two tackles for loss. For head coach Tim Lewis, whose primary experience is on the defensive side of the ball, the outcome was near perfection. "That was fantastic," Lewis said. "We tried to limit their explosive plays on defense and did a good job. Our third down defense was fantastic and I can't say enough about our kicker and punter (Colton Schmidt, who averaged 44 yards). Defensively we took the ball away a couple of times and made a couple of fourth down stops, and I consider those takeaways." The contest convinced me to devote a good portion of my site to the Alliance, and I even covered the Iron's road game against Atlanta on February 24, a game that came after Birmingham improved to 2-0 with a 12-9 win over Salt Lake.

The headline for me was seeing pro football teams from Birmingham and Atlanta meeting for the first time in history. But after I got settled in at Georgia State Stadium (formerly Turner Field), I realized it was the first time I'd seen a pro game involving a Magic City entry somewhere other than Legion Field. Regardless of locale it was another Birmingham victory – 28-12 – and I had fun watching the Iron improve to 3-0 on "enemy" turf. "I thought our guys ground it out and lived up to our name, Iron – I think we're a tough football team," Lewis said. "We're resilient, we're strong, we bend but we don't break. The guys did a fantastic job today."

Perez hit 17 of 31 passes for 160 yards and one interception in the win, and Quinton Patton led all Iron receivers with four catches for 58 yards. I was finally starting to adjust to the world of "farm club" football and buying into the concept. None of the guys on any of the teams had ever been NFL stars, although quite a few excelled in college and I was certain many would be back in the big leagues by 2020. The Iron hit a two-game skid in March, falling to San Antonio 12-11 and Orlando, 31-14. But they bounced back in one of the most entertaining games of the season, a 32-29 victory at San Diego. The Iron lost to Memphis 31-25 in overtime on March 24, and completed a sweep of Atlanta with a 17-9 victory at Legion Field on March 31. Yet the AAF was already looking like all the leagues that had come before it, and that look is "shaky."

It started when Carolina Hurricanes owner Tom Dundon invested $250 million in the league on February 19. Early reports suggested that money was needed to make payroll, but the spin was that it was merely Dundon's way of becoming part of a viable new professional sports league. His "gift" was so good he was made chairman and controlling owner of the league. By April 2, 2019, there was no league or chair to own. While Ebersol and co-founder Bill Polian were working behind the scenes to broker an official developmental deal with the NFL – one that would take some time – Dundon wasn't interested in waiting around. In March he publicly threatened to fold the league unless the NFL Players Association agreed to give the Alliance players on loan. The afternoon following April Fool's Day he proved his threat was more than just a cruel joke by pulling the plug on the league eight weeks into the season.

It was a unilateral move, and one that sent shockwaves throughout the league. Coaches like Spurrier said they were blindsided by the decision and felt they were lied to since the league was supposedly designed to last for three years without taking in any money. Officially the league "suspended operations," leaving a sliver of hope that perhaps it might still be salvaged. Each of the eight teams released statements later that night, however, making it clear the Alliance of American Football would never play another down. I received the news from the Iron – via email – at 8:14 p.m.

On behalf of all of us with the Birmingham Iron organization, we were shocked and incredibly disappointed to learn of the Boards' decision to suspend football operations.

Charlie Ebersol and Bill Polian delivered a quality football product that fans nationally were watching on TV, online, and here in Birmingham on each and every game day.

While all startups encounter some challenges, we believed ours could be addressed in the offseason, after a successful completion to our first season.

We were able to bring together rivals in the talent-rich state of Alabama, with players coming together in black, steel grey and silver. The Birmingham Iron promised a brand of football that made Alabama proud. We cannot thank our players, coaches, staff, corporate partners, and especially our fans that supported us from the moment our team was announced in the Magic City. The Birmingham community came together and proved to be some of the best fans in The Alliance.

We hope to be able to share information from The Alliance about ticket refunds in the future.

Thank you for your support and for believing in us.

Sincerely,

Tim Lewis, Head Coach

Joe Pendry, General Manager

A few days later, the Alliance issued its official statement: This week, we made the difficult decision to suspend all football operations for the Alliance of American Football. We understand the difficulty that this decision has caused for many people and for that we are very sorry. This is not the way we wanted it to end, but we are also committed to working on solutions for all outstanding issues to the best of our ability. Due to ongoing legal processes, we are unable to comment further or share details about the decision.

We are grateful to our players, who delivered quality football and may now exercise their NFL-out clauses in our contract. We encourage them to continue pursuing their dreams and wish them the best. We are grateful to our fans, who have been true believers from the beginning, and to our world-class partners. And to the Alliance coaches and employees who devoted their valuable time and considerable talent to this venture, we are forever grateful.

The end came just two days after Birmingham had clinched a playoff spot with its win over the Legends at Legion Field. The victory gave the Iron a 5-3 record, meaning they had wrapped up second place in the Eastern Conference and would face Orlando in the playoffs. The game against Atlanta was the last one they had scheduled for Legion Field and, indeed, the last one they would ever play.

On April 17, the Alliance of American Football filed for bankruptcy and officially went out of business.

"We are deeply disappointed to be taking this action. The AAF was created to be a dynamic, developmental professional football league powered by an unprecedented alliance between players, fans and the game. The AAF strove to create new opportunities for talented players, coaches, executives and officials while providing an exciting experience for fans. We are proud of the fact that our teams and players delivered on that goal. We thank our players, coaches and employees for their commitment to the game of football and to this venture. Our fans believed in the AAF from the beginning, and we thank them for their support. We are hopeful that our players, coaches and others will find opportunities to pursue their football dreams in the future. The AAF is committed to ensuring that our bankruptcy proceeds in an efficient and orderly manner. Pursuant to the bankruptcy laws, a trustee will be empowered to resolve all matters related to the AAF's remaining assets and liabilities, including ongoing matters related to player contracts."

Knowing what we know now, had Dundon not come aboard it would've likely died after a couple of weeks instead of eight. In the bankruptcy filings we learned that the league claimed assets of $11.3 million and liabilities totaling $48.3 million. On the bright side, the league still had $536,160.68 in cash. (Just kidding ... there was no bright side). Throw in the fact that former employees and some players filed lawsuits against league officials (the word "fraud" seemed to come up a lot) and you're left with an organization that will ultimately be remembered for failing its workers, partners and fans. To say I was heartbroken would be an overstatement; I'd seen this movie many times before and was quite familiar with the ending. And even though Birmingham has built a reputation of supporting pro football, the Iron was seemingly always dealing with inclement weather issues and struggled at the gate. Its average attendance of 14,307 per game was the lowest of all the gridiron leagues Birmingham had been a part of before, and the Iron's biggest crowd was 17,328 – that coming in its final contest. I was sad for the players, coaches and all the league personnel who lost their jobs, of course, but deep down I knew that any pro football organization other than the National Football League is living on borrowed time. Even so, the time was up on the Iron much more quickly than I imagined. And even though it didn't take long for me to embrace the team, it didn't take long for me to forget about it, either. I guess I'm just not as sentimental as I once was.

FULL TIME FAN AGAIN

Looking at it chronologically, that hot July night in Birmingham when I first saw the Birmingham Americans play seems like ancient history. It's jarring to think they debuted more than 40 years ago – way back in another century. It's even more jarring to know I debuted on the last day of 1960. I've led a very fortunate life, one that includes a long newspaper career that allowed me to not just follow sports closely, but get paid to write about it. How lucky is that? But as you might've guessed, my love for sports started long before I ever became a journalist, and continues now that I'm retired. And while it's taken a little time, I'm adjusting comfortably to being a "civilian" again. When it comes to football, UAB is my primary gridiron focus. That's where I graduated and where a good chunk of my parents' money went, so it's the team I have the most invested in. The fact that it has evolved into an outstanding Football Bowl Subdivision program doesn't hurt, either. As far as the NFL, I still pledge allegiance to the Jets (and also cheer for the Rams, now that they're back in Los Angeles). After the Houston Oilers moved to Nashville and became the Tennessee Titans, I found myself rooting for them to be successful, too. And living in South Carolina for the last 12 years has inspired me to follow the Carolina Panthers and Atlanta Falcons more closely. I even covered Panthers home games for a few seasons, which was a lot of fun and gave me a new appreciation for the National Football League.

As for the Americans, Vulcans, Stallions, and Barracudas – I still pine for those teams. I would've loved the WFL to have had owners with deep pockets and deeper commitments. Who knows? Wednesday night football might've become all the rage. And oh, how I wish USFL owners had listened to Bassett and kept a spring schedule. Top-level football throughout the year would've been fantastic. The bidding war with the NFL for players would've probably been too much over time and forced a merger, but I prefer to live in my spring fantasy world since we'll never know. Of course, if I could work my will and find Birmingham a permanent home in any pro league whose acronym is not NFL, it would be the CFL. I realize I'm in the minority there, but so be it. It's a gridiron hill I'm willing to die on. The Fire and Bolts never earned my devotion, and those are the most comparable teams and leagues to what the Magic City had with the Iron. I didn't let past opinions shape my outlook on Birmingham's latest team, though. I hoped they'd find a niche in my hometown. I hoped the league would take root and become a spring sports staple. More importantly, I hoped I'd never have to update this book with a chapter about the demise of yet another professional football team in Birmingham. But I did ... and I guess deep down I probably knew I would. That's only fitting, I suppose. After all, it's the teams of the past that inspired this book. And when I think about them – and I think about some of them more than I should – they'll always inspire me.

About the Author

Scott Adamson is a 30-year newspaper veteran who has covered everything from the NFL to the Masters. He has written sports and humor columns since 1987 and continues the tradition at his website, adamsonmedia.com.

9 780979 698897